The
Pentax
Guide

The Pentax Guide

A MODERN CAMERA GUIDE SERIES

Fred Swartz

AMPHOTO
American Photographic Book Publishing
An Imprint of Watson-Guptill Publications/New York

This book is dedicated to Grace and Will Connell.

Copyright © 1980 by Fred Swartz.

First published 1980 in New York by Amphoto,
American Photographic Book Publishing,
an imprint of Watson-Guptill Publications,
a division of Billboard Publications, Inc.,
1515 Broadway, New York, N.Y. 10036

Library of Congress Cataloging in Publication Data

Swartz, Fred.
  The Pentax guide.

  (A Modern camera guide series.)
  Includes index.
  1. Pentax camera.   2. Photography—Handbooks,
manuals, etc.   I. Title.   II. Series: Modern
camera guide series.
  TR263. P4S82   1980   771.3'1   80-17748

ISBN 0-8174-2471-7
ISBN 0-8174-2143-2 (pbk.)

Manufactured in U.S.A.

First Printing, 1980

2   3   4   5   6   7   8   9/86   85   84   83   82

Table of Contents

Acknowledgments

My sincere appreciation to Lou Jacobs, Jr. for his guidance and encouragement during a trying period.

To Mr. T. Akasu, International Advertising Manager, Asahi Optical Corporation, Tokyo, Japan. I am indebted for his assistance in checking the technical accuracy of my manuscript and for furnishing the technical reference material and most of the equipment photographs.

My thanks to Mr. David Plesser, V.P. Marketing, and Barry Goldberg, of the Pentax Corporation for the loan of Pentax System equipment.

To Mrs. Mary Edwards for her untiring efforts in coordinating communication with the New York, Colorado, and Japan offices of the Asahi Optical Corporation.

To Mrs. Patsy Schon, Sales and Service Administrator, and her assistant Ms. Patty Loyet, of the Pentax Factory Repair Center in West Los Angeles. With a special thanks to Richard Elliott, camera technician at the center for his technical advice and service.

To Allen's Custom Lab in Hollywood for their patience and fine work in developing and printing most of my black-and-white prints, to my specific instructions, used in this book.

To my family, friends, and colleagues for their moral support and encouragement.

To Amphoto editors Herb Taylor, Cora Marquez, Michael O'Connor who are responsible for the creative assembling and production of this book.

Most of the equipment photographs were furnished by the Asahi Optical Corporation and/or the manufacturer of the product shown. All of the others were taken by the author.

## CHAPTER 1

Evolution of the Pentax Single-Lens Reflex System

HISTORY OF THE COMPANY

The Asahi Optical Company was founded in 1919 as an eyeglass manufacturer. By 1923, they had expanded their operation into making camera lenses for the motion picture industry, the first ever made in Japan. A program sponsored by the Japanese government promoting the manufacture of cameras and lenses was started in 1931. This led Asahi to produce two unique lenses, an f/6.3 Opter and a 75 mm f/3.5. The company converted to the manufacture of wartime optical instruments, binoculars and rangefinders for the Manchurian war. From 1938, until the end of that war, Asahi produced aerial cameras. Binocular lenses became the prime export of the Japanese optical industry in 1948 and Asahi originated the micron-type binocular. Research on the development of a single-lens reflex (SLR) camera was started in 1945 and completed in 1951. Mass production of the first SLR designed and manufactured in Japan, the Asahiflex I, began in 1952.

EVOLUTION OF THE CAMERAS

The Asahiflex I was quite primitive by today's standards. It had a waist-level viewfinder located on top of the camera body. When the shutter was tripped, the mirror which reflected the image onto the ground glass lifted up out of the way. This caused the viewfinder to black out. It stayed that way until the film was advanced and the shutter cocked. Screw-mount lenses had to be wound into the camera body. Two years later Asahi brought out the Asahiflex IIB. It still had the waist-level finder but was equipped with a revolutionary feature, the instant-return mirror, which almost eliminated viewfinder blackout. This convenient feature was another first for Asahi and it is still an integral part of all 35 mm SLRs today.

Over the years the Asahi Optical Company has set an enviable record of firsts in the 35 mm SLR field. Many of their original, trend-setting, innovations have become standards still in use by the entire industry. Asahi's next major contribution to camera design was eye-level viewing. This was achieved in 1957 by using a pentaprism in the viewfinder. It was a true milestone in SLR development. It was at this point that the camera's name was changed to Pentax, which was derived from Pentaprism and Asahiflex.

Although the Pentax had the same basic structure as the Asahiflex it incorporated several design changes. In addition to the eye-level finder, a FResnel viewing screen gave added brightness to the viewfinder. The lens mount and flange were changed to standard international sizes. A light-alloy metal was used to give added strength to the lens mount. Camera operation was made easier through use of a lever-type film advance and a crank-type film rewind system. A whole new series

The Asahiflex 1 was the first 35 mm SLR both designed and built in Japan. It was placed on the market in 1952.

The first Asahi Pentax was introduced in 1957. It was a completely redesigned Asahiflex with an eye-level pentaprism and other improvements.

of screw-mount, interchangeable Takumar lenses and accessories for the Pentax were also released at this time. Adapters were made available so the new lenses could be used with the older Asahi lens mounts.

The next model was the original Pentax K, introduced in 1958, which came with a newly developed lens. This lens, the Auto Takumar standard lens, was made with a new type of optical glass. In addition, this lens had built-in semi-automatic aperture control, which made possible focusing at the largest aperture opening. Focusing was also made easier through use of a microprism grid in the center of the finder. The Pentax K had a top shutter speed of 1/1000th of a second. The Pentax and the Pentax K gained international popularity, and were sold in the United States by Sears bearing their Tower nameplate.

Asahi Pentax cameras were distributed by the Heiland Company for a brief period during 1959 in this country and these cameras had a Heiland Pentax nameplate. The nameplate changed to Honeywell Pentax after the Minneapolis-Honeywell Corporation purchased the Heiland Company. Pentax cameras sold in other parts of the world had the Asahi Pentax nameplate. Starting with the most recent K and M series, all Pentax cameras will now have the Asahi Pentax nameplates no matter where they are sold.

In 1959, the first of the Pentax S-series cameras, the S2, was released. This was the first Pentax to combine all shutter speed settings on a one-axis, non-rotating dial on top of the camera. It also had a ready-to-go indicator near the shutter release. A red dot could be seen after the film was advanced and the shutter cocked. The shutter speed range was from 1 second to 1/500th of a second. This was followed by the Pentax S3 two years later featuring another Asahi first, a clip-on exposure meter, that used a CdS photocell to measure light. The meter was mounted by clipping it to the eyepiece frame, and became operational when the meter pin was inserted into a small groove on the shutter speed dial. The new standard lens for the S3 had fully automatic aperture control, which meant that after the exposure was made, the lens returned to its maximum aperture. You no longer had to open the aperture manually after exposure, as was nec-

The Asahi Pentax K (above) was released in 1958. It had three new features: semi-automatic diaphragm control, a 1/1000 sec. shutter speed, and a microprism focusing grid.

The Pentax S2 (above right) was released in 1959. It had the first shutter-cocked indicator. This camera was first sold in the U.S. as the Heiland Pentax H-1 and later as the Honeywell Pentax H-1.

The Asahi Pentax S3 (right) was introduced in 1960. It had the first fully automatic-diaphragm lens, and a clip-on exposure meter.

essary with the semi-automatic lenses. The Pentax SV which followed in 1962, had the first self-timer ever incorporated into a camera body.

Another classic feature pioneered by Asahi and later adopted by most SLR manufacturers was through-the-lens metering (TTL). The prototype of the Pentax Spotmatic with TTL created quite a sensation when it was first shown at the 1960 Photokina trade show in West Germany. Four more years of testing and redesigning were necessary before Asahi engineers approved the release of the first Spotmatic in 1964. They had met the challenge of incorporating a metering system without increasing the size or weight of the camera. This was in contrast to other SLR manufacturers whose cameras were getting larger, heavier, and bulkier. The popularity of the Spotmatic pushed the total production figures of all Pentax cameras past the one million mark by mid-1966, just fourteen years after their introduction. On an esoteric note, a speciality camera for taking long-distance pictures by infrared light at night, the Pentax Nocta, was intro-

Asahi's classic creation was the Spotmatic with its through-the-lens metering system. This was the first metering system to use a Cds cell. The Spotmatic was placed on the market in 1964.

duced in 1966. This was an SV-type camera, and was especially useful in recording the habits and life modes of nocturnal animals.

In 1967, a motor-drive system was introduced for the Spotmatic, making it even more popular. This drive could be used for continuous-sequence exposures at 2.5 to 3 frames per second at shutter speeds from 1/60th through 1/1000th of a second. Single-frame exposures were possible at speeds from one second through 1/1000th second. It provided for wireless remote-control operation and the taking of up to 250 continuous exposures through use of an automatic timer and special back. Asahi was awarded the German Good Design of the Year Award for the motor drive. It was the first time this award was given to a Japanese product.

Two more firsts were scored by Asahi in 1971. Super-multi-layer coating of their Takumar lenses was achieved by developing a technique for ap-

plying seven separate layers to the surface of each lens. This kept surface reflections to a minimum and helped eliminate lens flare and ghost images. There also was a major gain in light transmission. Tests showed a twenty percent improvement in Gauss-type standard lenses and a whopping gain of fifty percent in zoom lenses. There were also great improvements in the clarity of color tone, better contrast and greater brightness, all of which give us better picture quality today.

Asahi's other enviable innovation in 1971 was the world's first fully automatic-exposure 35 mm SLR, the Pentax ES. The ES had an electronic shutter which was controlled by an aperture-preferred automatic system. You set the lens aperture and the control system set the correct shutter speed, right up to the exact moment of exposure. It had a choice of shutter speeds from one full second through 1/1000th of a second. Asahi provided manual override of the automatic system with 4×,

2×, 1× and 1/2× settings. This permitted adjustment for back-lit subjects and extremely contrasty situations.

The parade of Pentax models continued in 1973 with the introduction of the Spotmatic F and the ES II. This Spotmatic was an improved version with a through-the-lens open-aperture metering system, a hot shoe for flash on top of the prism and a shutter-release lock. The ES II was an advanced model of the ES, with an increased shutter-speed range of 8 full seconds through 1/1000th of a second, a self-timer and a built-in viewfinder cover. An economy version of the Spotmatic, the SP 1000 was released in 1974. In this model several features were eliminated, including the hot shoe, the self-timer, the shutter-button lock. Only stop-down metering was provided.

TODAY'S MODELS

Asahi's current Pentax cameras are the K and M series. The K series marked a basic change in Pentax design, from the screw-thread mount to bayonet-mount lenses. Three models, the K2, KX, and KM, were introduced in 1975, along with a new series of 26 SMC lenses and a complete line of accessories. Two more models, the K 1000 and the K2DMD, were released a year later. All of

Asahi introduced the first fully automatic-exposure 35 mm SLR with an aperture-preferred system in 1971. This camera was the Pentax ES.

Pentax released the incredibly small and lightweight MX (left) and ME (right) in 1977. At the same time Pentax released a new series of compact bayonet-mount lenses, the SMC Pentax-M lenses.

these are described in detail later in this book. The M series followed in 1977 with two models, the fully automatic ME, and the MX which is billed as the world's smallest, lightest, and most compact, full-featured SLR. They are discussed in depth later in the book.

Asahi Pentax's newest 35mm SLR camera (introduced in 1980) is the LX. This camera is designed to meet the specific needs of professional and advanced amateur photographers. It offers a choice of aperture-preferred automatic exposure or completely manual exposure control, and uses a "Integrated Direct Metering" (IDM) system which measures the light hitting the shutter curtain and film. There is a complete line of accessory equipment available for this camera, including interchangeable focusing screens and viewfinders, a data back and motor drive, and various dedicated electronic flash units.

The popularity of Pentax cameras has proven true the philosophy of the Asahi Optical Company's founder Kumao Kajiwara: "To manufacture original products of excellent quality—creatively, efficiently and at reasonable cost." Although it took fourteen years, starting with the first camera built by Asahi, to pass the one-million production mark, it was only three years later in 1969, that production topped two million. In just two more years, they had reached the three million mark. There were over six million Pentax cameras in use in 1976 and, as you read further, it will become evident why these cameras are so popular.

## CHAPTER 2

The Pentax K Series

More than ten years of planning and production were invested in the creation of the Asahi Pentax K-series system. It marked a major change in Pentax design, from screw-mount lenses to the much more convenient, bayonet-mount lenses. There are five models in the current K series. The K2, KX, and KM were introduced in 1975, and the K2DMD and the K1000 followed in 1976. Asahi's engineers also designed a new group of 16 open-aperture, interchangeable, SMC Pentax K lenses and a comprehensive set of accessories to complete the system. You also have a choice of 24 SMC Pentax M mini-lenses, which were introduced in 1977 for the compact M-series system. They have the same bayonet mount and are interchangeable with K-series camera bodies. In addition, the older Pentax screw-mount lenses can be used with Mount Adapter B and stop-down metering. The K-series models have a number of common characteristics, but they are distinctly different cameras. Use the chart comparing these cameras in order to choose the best camera for your personal needs.

The K-series cameras—the K2 (shown here), KX, KM, K2DMD, and K 1000—were ten years in the planning and marked a major design change for Pentax. With these cameras Pentax changed from screw-mount lenses to the more practical bayonet-mount lenses.

THE K2

The most advanced models of the K series are the K2 and the K2DMD. They have many of the same features and use the same camera body. First we will take a comprehensive look at the K2 and later discuss the additional features of the K2DMD.

Asahi's basic policy of keeping their equipment as compact and as light as possible, is followed in their design of the K-series cameras. The K2 with a 50 mm f/1.4 lens, measures but 144 mm × 92 mm x 94 mm (5.7 × 3.6 × 3.7), and weighs just 946 g (33.7 oz.).

(Editorial note: Production of the Pentax K2 was discontinued in June of 1980, but new models of this camera are expected to be available for some time to come. Used models will probably be available for years at a good price. The K2DMD is still being manufactured as of this writing.)

PENTAX K2 SPECIFICATIONS

Type: 35 mm SLR with through-the-lens light meter and vertical electronic focal-plane shutter. Exposure control fully automatic or manual.

Film and picture size: 35 mm film. 24 mm × 36 mm.

Standard lenses: SMC Pentax 50 mm f/1.2, 50 mm f/1.4, and 55 mm f/1.8 with fully-automatic diaphragm. Minimum aperture: f/22. Filter size: 52 mm. Focusing: 0.45 m (1.5 ft.) to infinity.

Shutter: Vertical-run, metal focal-plane shutter. Shutter-button lock provided. Automatic electronic shutter: stepless between 8 and 1/1000 sec. Manual electronic shutter: 8, 4, 2, 1, 1/2, 1/4, 1/8, 1/15, 1/30, 1/60, 1/125, 1/250, 1/500, 1/1000 sec. Manual mechanical shutter: B, 1/125 and 1/1000 sec. (when battery is dead.)

Flash synchronization: X-contact hot-shoe for cordless flash connection. FP + X contact for conventional flash cord connection. X synchronization at 1/125 sec.

Self-timer: Built-in self-timer with interrupt function. 5-9 sec. delay after tripping shutter release.

Viewfinder: Pentaprism finder with cross-microprism or split-image focusing screen. 0.88× magnification with 50 mm lenses (life-size with 55 mm lens). 95% field of view. Dioptry −0.8. "Incorrect exposure range" indicator.

Focusing: Microprism and split-image screens standard, plus custom screens.

Reflex mirror: Swing-up-and-back, instant-return type, with mirror-lock-up lever, and special shock absorbers for minimum vibration.

Film advance: Single-stroke wind lever. 25-degree pre-advance and 130-degree advance angles.

Exposure counter: Automatic re-set.

Film rewind: Rapid-rewind crank lifts clear of body.

Lens mount: Pentax bayonet mount. Rotation: 65-degrees.

Exposure meter: Silicon-Photo-Diode-activated, aperture-preferred meter measures the entire area of ground glass with emphasis on central portion at full lens aperture. Match needles for correct exposure on manual. Couples directly to shutter, aperture, and film speed settings. Shutter speed and auto/manual setting visible in viewfinder for exposure doublecheck.

Exposure control: Exposure factor control dial: 4×, 2×, 1×, 1/2×, 1/4× for specific exposure control.

Power source: Two 1.5-volt silver-oxide batteries (Eveready S76E or Mallory MS76H).

Meter switch: Meter goes ON when shutter button is depressed halfway. Also, when film-wind lever is at its pre-advance angle and shutter button is depressed halfway, meter stays ON. Battery check button and lamp provided.

Dimensions: With 50 mm f/1.4 lens: width 144 mm (5.7″) × height 92 mm (3.6″) × depth 94 mm (3.7″).

Weight: 946 g (33.7 ozs.) with 50 mm f/1.4 lens. 680 g (24.2 ozs.) with no lens.

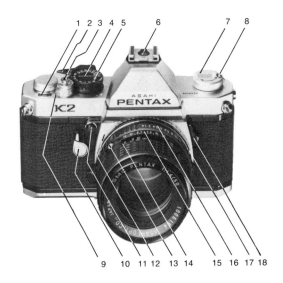

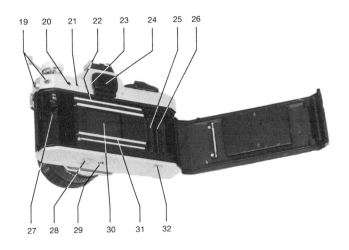

PENTAX K2—PARTS NOMENCLATURE

1. Frame counter
2. Film-advance lever
3. Shutter-release button
4. Shutter-speed dial
5. Shutter-speed-dial-lock release
6. Hot shoe
7. Film-rewind/back-cover-release knob
8. Film-rewind crank
9. Shutter-button-lock lever
10. Self-timer lever

11. Depth-of-field-preview lever
12. Exposure-compensation ring
13. Upraised lens-alignment dot
14. Distance scale
15. Depth-of-field scale
16. Aperture ring
17. ASA film-speed ring
18. Mirror-lock-up lever
19. Flash-sync terminals
20. Battery-check button
21. Battery-check lamp

22. Film-guide rail
23. Accessory fitting groove
24. Viewfinder eyepiece
25. Film-sprocket spool
26. Film-takeup spool
27. Film-cartridge chamber
28. Battery-chamber cover
29. Tripod socket
30. Shutter curtain
31. Film rail
32. Film-rewind button

Viewing and Focusing

Viewing and focusing have been greatly improved over past models by applying a new silver coating to the reflective surface of the pentaprism. This gives you a much brighter image in the viewfinder.

Another plus is the deeply recessed eyepiece, which helps keep the viewing lens from smudging and having to be cleaned too often. There is a problem however, if you wear glasses. Since your eye is not close enough to the finder window, you lose over 25 percent of one side of the screen because of the tendency to favor the side with the meter needle. There is a solution: diopter-correction lens adapters are available from −3 to +2.

Two focusing screens are standard with the K2: a microprism spot, or a split-image, rangefinder spot. Decide which type you prefer before you buy the camera, the screens can only be changed by a Pentax service center. Asahi has eliminated the problem of mirror-cut-off with long-telephoto lenses through use of a large instant-return mirror which swings up-and-back, out of the way. The depth-of-field preview button can be operated by the second finger, without taking the forefinger off the shutter release.

Exposure Control

The K2 has two types of exposure control. It can be either fully automatic with open-aperture metering, or manual with match-needle operation. Older, screw-mount Pentax Takumar lenses and certain older accessories can be used with an adapter, but stop-down metering is required. The metering system uses a silicon photo-diode with almost instant response and good stability. It is of the center-weighted type, measuring all of the ground glass but emphasizing the central portion.

To activate the camera's metering system for a short period of time, press the shutter-release button part way. The meter will turn off when you release the button. Should you wish the meter to stay on, first pull the rapid-wind lever out to the pre-advance position (about 25 degrees away from the camera body), then press the shutter-release button part way. The meter will stay on until you return the rapid-wind lever to the closed position. There is also a shutter-release-lock lever on the collar around the shutter-release button to provide insurance against depletion of the batteries, or accidental firing of the camera.

On the right side of the viewing screen is a vertical list of shutter speeds from 1/1000 sec. to 8

This is the standard microprism-spot focusing system of the K2. A split-image, rangefinder type is also available, but it must be ordered when you purchase the camera.

To change the K2 camera's operating mode from automatic to manual, press the small release button on top of the shutter-speed dial and turn the dial to the desired shutter speed.

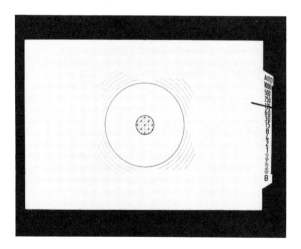

The exposure-factor control provides exposure compensation up to plus or minus two stops. This compensation is especially handy in high-contrast or backlighted situations.

seconds. *Auto* (for automatic exposure) is at the top and *B* (for bulb, or time exposure) is at the bottom of the scale. Two needles can also be seen, a thick translucent-blue one and a thin black one. When you set the shutter-speed dial to *AUTOMATIC,* the black needle is the working indicator, and the blue needle locks into place at *Auto.* As you change the aperture, the black needle moves to indicate the shutter speeds the camera's automatic-exposure system has chosen.

To change to manual operation simply press the small button on the shutter-speed dial and turn the dial to the desired shutter speed. The blue needle inside the viewfinder will then move to indicate that shutter-speed setting. Match the black needle to the blue one by adjusting the aperture ring, or the shutter speed to get the proper exposure.

A method of adjusting automatic exposure for extreme-lighting or background-contrast situations is provided by the exposure-factor-control ring. This ring circles the lens mount along with the ASA film-speed-dial ring. Looking down at the top of the camera, the ASA speeds are on the left and the exposure-factor-control settings are on the right.

The exposure-factor control provides exposure compensation up to plus or minus two stops. Changes made with this control are shown in the viewfinder by the black needle.

Shutter System

The Pentax K2 uses the Seiko MF (metal focal-plane) electronically controlled shutter. This was developed jointly by Asahi and Seiko for the K2. Unlike conventional focal-plane shutters which move horizontally, the Seiko MF has five metal leaves which drop vertically. This system is very durable, and allows electronic-flash synchronization at shutter speeds up to 1/125 of a second. This faster-than-normal shutter speed helps eliminate ghost images, and also makes the use of flash fill easier.

When the camera is set in automatic mode, shutter speeds are stepless. It will choose times between conventional shutter speeds to suit the exact lighting situation. In manual mode there are 14 conventional, electronically controlled shutter speeds. When the battery is weak, the electronic

This gnarled, interestingly shaped tree (above) fascinated me, but was a disappointing subject during the day because of the busy background. A time exposure at night provided the answer. The exposure-factor control was used to cut back the overexposure that would have resulted from an automatic reading of the black background.

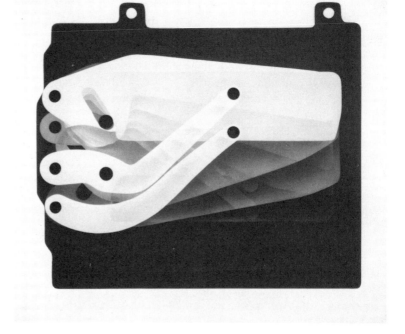

Diagram (right) of the vertical-drop, metal, focal-plane shutter developed for the K2 camera by Asahi and Seiko. Electronically controlled, it has stepless speeds in automatic mode.

shutter and metering system stop working. Asahi has provided three mechanical speeds for such an emergency: B, 1/125 sec. and 1/1000 sec. Even so, it is a good idea to carry an extra set of batteries, especially when traveling, so your K2 will be able to deliver its full shutter-speed range.

Mirror Lock-Up

The instant-return mirror, which reflects the image onto the ground glass, swings up out of the way during exposure. It drops back into place immediately after the film has been exposed. This can cause a certain amount of vibration, which is not usually too noticeable when using short-focal-length lenses. However, any vibration can become pronounced when using long telephoto lenses or shooting extreme close-ups. To avoid this, theKX, K2, and K2DMD provide mirror lock-up. The lock-up lever is on the upper-left side of the lens mount and lifts the mirror up out of the way. The mirror stays that way until you return the lever to its origi-nal position. Focusing and exposure readings must be made before locking up the mirror because the viewfinder blacks out once it is up. Manual mode must be used since auto mode cannot operate without the mirror.

Self-timer

The self-timer can be helpful to prevent jarring the camera while tripping the shutter, as well as for getting yourself into the photograph. The self-timer delays the release of the shutter from 5 to 9 seconds, depending on how far down you push the lever. The self-timer functions both in manual and automatic modes, but one precaution must be taken when the camera is in automatic mode and your eye is away from the viewfinder. Light entering through the eyepiece can cause errors in exposure. This can be prevented by sliding an accessory cap over the eyepiece, thus shielding the metering system from extraneous light.

To set the self-timer (below), turn the self-timer lever counterclockwise as far as you wish. (It will delay the release of the shutter from five to nine seconds, depending how far you turn it.) To activate the self-timer, push the camera's shutter-release button. The self-timer can be cancelled by returning the lever to its normal position before the shutter-release button is pressed.

To lock the mirror up out of the way during long exposures, or when shooting extreme close-ups, push the lock-up lever (on the upper-left side of the lens mount) up. The mirror will remain locked up until you return the lever to its normal position.

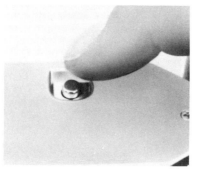

To make multiple exposures with the Pentax K2 follow these five steps: 1) Make the first exposure normally. 2) Turn the film-rewind knob clockwise until the film feels taut, and hold it there. 3) While still holding the rewind knob, depress the film-release button on the bottom of the camera. 4) After depressing the film-release button, advance the rapid-wind lever in the normal fashion to cock the shutter. 5) Make the next exposure.

Electrical System

Pentax K-series cameras are powered by two 1.5 V silver-oxide batteries (Eveready S76E or Mallory MS76H). These should last you about a year with average use. I replace mine about every six months to be on the safe side, and carry an extra set on extended trips. There is a battery-check button on the left side of the back of the camera, below the rewind knob. To use it, press the button and the lamp next to it should glow brightly. If the lamp doesn't glow, then the batteries must be replaced.

Flash Synchronization

Flashes can be synchronized with the cameras in two ways. All K-series cameras have a built-in hot-shoe on top of the pentaprism. It has a built-in X contact for electronic flash which remains off until an electronic-flash unit is mounted on the shoe. This eliminates the danger of electric shocks when the hot-shoe is not in use. There are also separate X and FP terminals located near the film-rewind knob. These should be used for flashes with cord connections. The X terminal synchronizes with electronic flashes at speeds up to 1/125 sec. and with M, MF, and MP-class flashbulbs at speeds up to 1/15 sec. Sync with FP-class bulbs is possible on all shutter speeds. These terminals should be kept covered when not in use.

Multiple Exposures

Multiple exposures can be made with the K2, but there is no separate control for this technique. To make a multiple exposure, use the following procedure:

1. Make your first exposure.
2. Turn the rewind knob gently, until the film feels taut and hold it there.
3. While holding the rewind knob, push the film-rewind button, on the base of the camera, while cocking the rapid-wind lever.

You have now cocked the shutter without moving the film and are ready to make the second exposure on the same frame. Follow this procedure for as many exposures as you wish. After making the final exposure, it is a good idea to cover the lens and make a blank exposure before continuing to take additional pictures. This will help avoid overlapping with the following photographs if the registration is not exact. It will take some experimentation with exposure settings to get the result you want. For double exposures, a good starting place is to either double your film-speed rating, or use twice the normal shutter speed on each exposure. Proceed from there. Normal exposure settings can be used if your subjects are in front of a black background.

This photograph is a double exposure. The first image was made with the model posed against the sky, and was shot at about half the exposure called for by the meter. The second image was made with the model posed in front of a dark rock formation, and was again photographed at half the normal exposure.

THE K2DMD

As stated earlier in this chapter, the K2 and K2DMD have the same size camera bodies and many of the same features. But, there are some important differences, and we will now discuss these differences specifically.

Viewing and Focusing

The standard focusing screen for the K2DMD is a three-way focusing system. It consists of a split-image, rangefinder spot in the center of the screen, surrounded by a microprism collar. Both are set into a ground-glass screen. This combination should fulfill just about any focusing need.

An aperture-read-out window is visible in the top center of the viewfinder, just above the viewing screen. This window shows the aperture in use with all SMC Pentax lenses, except the Shift f/3.5. This aperture-read-out window changes color, from white to orange, when the exposure-factor control has been moved. This is a helpful reminder to change the exposure-factor control back to its normal position after use.

The K2DMD also has a built-in eyepiece blind which eliminates the need of carrying an separate viewfinder cap. To close the built-in eye-piece blind, and prevent exposure error when the camera is on automatic and your eye is away from the viewfinder, turn the shutter-speed dial to the rectangle next to *AUTOMATIC*.

23

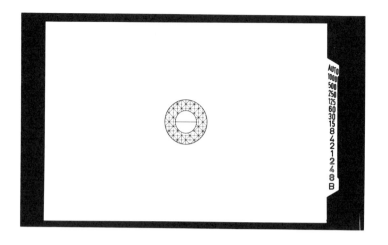

A three-way focusing screen (above) is standard for the K2DMD. This screen has a split-image, rangefinder spot in the center surrounded by a microprism ring. Both the split-image spot and microprism ring are set into a groundglass field. This combination of focusing systems will handle just about any conditions.

There is a built-in eyepiece blind in the K2DMD (above right). This blind eliminates stray light which might influence the meter when using the camera in automatic mode with your eye away from the viewfinder. The blind is moved into place by aligning the rectangle on the shutter-speed dial with the triangular index mark on the camera body (right).

PENTAX K2 DMD SPECIFICATIONS

Camera type: Aperture-Priority AE 35 mm SLR with manual override and provision for motor drive.

Shutter: Electronically controlled Seiko MF vertically moving, metal focal-plane shutter.
  Auto: Stepless range of 1/1000-8 seconds.
  Manual: 1/1000-8 seconds & B.
  Mechanical Shutter: B, 1/125 sec. (no batteries and dial set to 1/125-1 sec.), 1/1000 sec. (no batteries and dail set to 1/1000-1/250 sec.).

Synchronization: Hot-shoe with built-in circuit breaker, FP and X threaded terminals, X-sync at 1/125 sec.

Self-timer: 5-9 sec. delay, starts with shutter-release button, can be stopped while operating and bypassed.

Viewfinder: Silvered pentaprism for brilliant viewing, split-micro focusing aid, magnification of .88× with 50 mm lens at infinity, 95% of picture taking area visible, eyepiece of −.8 diopter, built-in eyepiece blind. Auto/manual indicator, aperture, shutter-speed indicator for both auto and manual operation, and exposure-compensation warning visible in viewfinder. Match-needle operation possible for manual exposure control.

Mirror: Extra-large, swing-back mirror for elimination of mirror cut-off and with provision for mirror lock-up.

Exposure measurement: Silicon Photo Diode open-aperture, center-weighted through-the-lens exposure measurement for aperture-priority AE or match-needle manual exposure control. ±2 EV exposure compensation provision, exposure-memory lock (automatic exposure temporarily memorized when mirror-lock-up lever is held downward or memorized approximately 10 minutes when mirror is locked in the upraised position), exposure measurement range of EV 1-18 (f/1.4 lens, 100 ASA) ASA range of 8-6400, meter switch incorporated into film-advance lever and shutter-release button.

Film advance: Plastic thumb grip, single stroke, 135-degree throw with stand-off angle of 25 degree.

Exposure counter: Additive type with automatic reset.

Film rewind: Rapid-rewind crank built into rewind knob.

Lens mount: Pentax K Bayonet Mount.

Power source: Two 1.5-volt silver-oxide batteries which last approximately one year with normal use, battery-check lamp (LED) to test battery condition, automatic "shutter-lock" when attempting to use camera with batteries of insufficient voltage, serving as warning to replace batteries.

Back cover: Back cover has built-on film tab holder and is interchangeable with data back, opens by pulling up rewind knob.

Built-in coupling: Shutter-release pin, film-transport coupler, and direct contact terminals which couple to motor drive. Built-in data-light-shield which couples to data switch, and direct contact terminal which couples to data back.

Dimensions: 144 mm (5.8 in.) × 92 mm (3.7 in.) × 90.4 mm (3.6 in.) (with 50 mm f/1.4 lens).

Weight: 953 g (34 oz.) (with 50 mm f/1.4 lens), 688 g (24.5 oz.) (without lens and batteries).

Additional features: Built-on tripod socket, depth-of-field-preview button, lenses provided with upraised dots for instant matching and mounting to camera body, reinforced neck strap lugs, all back body, texturized body surface for sure grip.

Exposure Control

An exposure-memory lock is incorporated into the mirror-lock-up lever of the K2DMD. This enables you to take an exposure reading in automatic mode, lock-in that reading, move your position, and than take the picture with the programmed reading. This is particularly useful in extreme-contrast conditions, such as when your subject is back lit. If you are taking a portrait you can move in close to your subject and take a close-up exposure reading of the face. To hold that reading, press down on the mirror-lock-up lever; this will hold the reading and lock the shutter-speed needle in place. The exposure will remain the same as long as the lever is held down, or until you have made the exposure. You can also retain the automatic-exposure setting for up to ten minutes by locking up the mirror.

Another method of obtaining accurate exposure in high-contrast conditions is to take readings of alternate subjects, such as the palm of your hand. When shooting landscapes where the sky is

The K2DMD has an exposure-memory lock incorporated into the mirror-lock-up lever. This control permits you to take an exposure reading with the camera on *Automatic,* change the composition of the photograph, and hold the initial reading until the shutter is fired. This feature is particularly useful with back-lit subjects, such as next photograph. The exposure-memory lock is activated by holding the mirror-lock-up lever down.

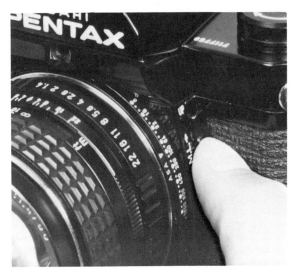

This photograph was taken using the exposure-memory lock and the camera set on *Automatic*. Had I used the exposure the meter recommended for this photograph the model would have been underexposed because of the intense back light. Instead I moved close to the model and took a reading of only her. Then I held this reading with the exposure-memory lock, backed up, and took the photograph.

predominant, point the camera down at an angle to exclude some of the sky, and use the exposure-memory lock procedure.

Electrical System

The K2DMD has a low-battery-voltage warning system in addition to its battery check. This prevents errors in exposure when battery voltage drops below the level needed for the camera to function accurately. The low-battery-voltage warning system causes the shutter to lock automatically after it is fired. In addition, the film-advance lever cannot be moved and the instant-return mirror stays in the up position, blacking out the viewfinder. At this point the battery-check light will not light up, showing that the batteries are used up. To return the camera to normal functioning, turn the shutter-speed dial to *B* for a short time. This will drain the remaining voltage left in the batteries, so the mirror will drop back down and the shutter will unlock. Then replace the dead batteries with new ones and you are ready to go again.

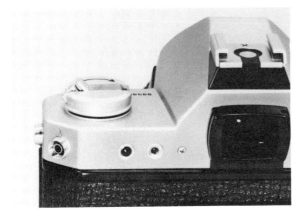

The K2DMD has a battery-check feature (left). If the batteries have enough power, the small diode behind the film-rewind knob will light up when the button next to it is pressed.

The K2DMD becomes a data-imprinting camera by replacing the standard back with the accessory Data Back MD (right). This accessory back has a built-in watch which imprints the date, hour, minute, and second the photograph was taken on the upper-left corner of the film frame.

Data Back MD

You can convert the K2DMD into a data-imprinting camera by replacing the standard camera back with the accessory data-back MD.

The data-back MD has a built-in clock showing the day of the month, hour, minute, and second. There is also an area for penciling in additional information. The clock is removable for easy setting and winding. Once it is mounted and turned on the clock face automatically appears as a 3.8 mm circle in the upper-left-hand corner of the film frame. The data back can be used with or without the motor drive, and can be switched off when imprinting is not desired. This unit has its own power source, and includes a battery check which flashes to verify consistent operation.

THE K1000

The K1000 is a modernized, bayonet-mount, version of the Spotmatic F. Like the SP1000, this is an economy model with fewer features, but offering the same reliable, precision construction of other Pentax products. The K1000 is a good choice for those who want a camera that is simple to operate, with no sacrifice in the quality of prints and slides.

The following features are not provided: Self-timer, depth-of-field preview, FP-sync terminal on the camera body (there is an X-sync terminal and a hot-shoe for electronic flash), mirror lock-up, and shutter-release lock.

The K1000 has a CdS exposure meter which measures the overall, average brightness of the ground glass at open aperture. Meter readout is of the center-needle type, observable in the view-finder.

To set the ASA, first push the small black knob on the innermost ring just below the ASA numbers. Then, while holding the knob in, move the knurled ring just below the knob until the ASA-indicator triangle points to the desired ASA setting.

Since the controls for the exposure-factor control and the ASA setting are on the same ring encircling the lens mount their operation can become confusing. The key point to remember is that the exposure-factor control should be at its normal setting of *1X* when you change the ASA setting.

PENTAX K1000 SPECIFICATIONS

Type: 35 mm SLR with built-in through-the-lens exposure meter.

Film and negative size: 35 mm film. 24 mm × 36 mm negative size.

Standard lens: SMC Pentax-M 50 mm f/2 with fully-automatic diaphragm. Filter size: 49 mm. Minimum focusing distance: 45 cm.

Shutter: Rubberized-silk focal-plane shutter. Speeds: B, 1 to 1/1000 sec.

Viewfinder: Pentaprism finder with cross-microprism or split-image focusing screen. 0.88× magnification with 50 mm standard lens focused at infinity. Dioptry −1.0.

Reflex mirror: Instant-return type with special shock absorbers for minimum vibration.

Lens mount: Pentax bayonet mount.

Film advance: Ratchet-type rapid-wind lever. 160-degree throw and 10-degree play. "Cocked" indicator alongside shutter-release button.

Exposure counter: Automatic reset.

Film rewind: Rapid-rewind crank for speedy film take-up.

Flash synchronization: X contact hot-shoe for cordless flash connection. X synchronization at 1/60 sec.

Exposure meter: CdS meter measures the average brightness of the ground glass at full aperture, and couples directly to aperture, shutter, and film-speed settings. Zero-method exposure control. Film speed from 20 to 3200 ASA. EV 3-18 with ASA 100 film. Powered with one 1.5-volt silver-oxide battery. Built-in photoswitch.

Dimensions: With 50 mm f/2 lens: width 143 mm (5.6″) × height 91.4 mm (3.6″) × 83 mm (3.3″)

Weight: 790 g (27.7 ozs.) with 50 mm f/2 lens. 620 g (21.7 ozs.) without lens.

THE KM AND KX

Both the KM and the KX have been phased out of the Pentax line. Although they were fine cameras, the company felt that the KM and the K1000, and the KX and the MX, were too close to continue marketing all four cameras. I have included specifications for the KM and KX as background for those of you who might be interested in purchasing a used model of these cameras, or who already own one. In the next chapter we will take a close look at the fully automatic ME, and the world's smallest, lightest, and most compact full-featured single-lens reflex camera, the Pentax MX.

PENTAX KX SPECIFICATIONS

Type: 35 mm SLR with built-in through-the-lens exposure meter.

Film and negative size: 35 mm film. 24 mm × 36 mm negative size.

Standard lenses: SMC Pentax 50 mm f/1.2, 50 mm f/1.4 and 55 mm f/1.8 with fully-automatic diaphragm. Filter size: 52 mm. Focusing: 0.45 m (1.5 ft.) to infinity.

Shutter: Horizontal-run, focal-plane shutter of rubberized-silk curtains. Speeds: B, 1 to 1/1000 sec.

Self-timer: Built-in self-timer with interrupt function. Releases shutter in 5-13 sec.

Viewfinder: Pentaprism finder with cross-microprism or split-image focusing screen. 0.87× magnification with 50 mm lenses (life-size with 55 mm lens). Dioptry −1.0.

Focusing: Turn focusing ring until viewfinder image comes into focus.

Reflex mirror: Instant-return type with special shock absorbers for minimum vibration.

Lens mount: Pentax bayonet mount.

Film advance: Ratchet-type rapid-wind lever. 10-degree pre-advance angle and 160-degree advance angle. "Cocked" indicator alongside shutter release button.

Exposure counter: Automatic reset.

Film rewind: Rapid-rewind crank for speedy film take-up.

Flash synchronization: X contact hot-shoe for cordless flash connection. FP + X contacts for conventional flash cord connection. X synchronization at 1/60 sec.

Exposure meter: CdS meter measures the average brightness of the ground glass at full aperture, and couples directly to aperture, shutter, and film-speed settings. Center needle for correct exposures. Film speed from 20 to 3200 ASA. EV 3-18 for ASA 100 film with 50 mm lens. Powered with one 1.5-volt silver-oxide battery.

Loaded-film indicator: Reminder dial below film-rewind knob, with settings for 20 or 36 (exposures), and the type of film in use.

Dimensions: With 50 mm f/1.4 lens: width 143 mm (5.6″) × height 91.4 mm (3.6″) × depth 94 mm (3.7″).

Weight: 887 g (31 ozs.) with 50 mm f/1.4 lens. 622 g (21.8 ozs.) with no lens.

PENTAX KM SPECIFICATIONS

Type: 35 mm SLR with built-in through-the-lens exposure meter.

Film and negative size: 35 mm film. 24 mm × 36 mm negative size.

Standard lenses: SMC Pentax 50 mm f/1.2, 50 mm f/1.4, and 55 mm f/1.8 with fully-automatic diaphragm. Filter size: 52 mm. Minimum aperture: f/22. Focusing: 0.45 mm (1.5 ft.) to infinity.

Shutter: Horizontal-run, focal-plane shutter of rubberized-silk curtains. Speeds: B, 1-1/1000 sec. Shutter-button lock provided.

Self-timer: Built-in self-timer with interrupt function. Releases shutter in 5-13 sec.

Viewfinder: Pentaprism finder with cross-microprism or split-image focusing screen. Aperture setting on lens visible in viewfinder. Shutter-speed setting indicated by blue needle. 0.88× magnification with 50 mm lenses (life-size with 55 mm lens). Dioptry −0.8. 93% field of view.

Focusing: Turn focusing ring until viewfinder image comes into focus.

Reflex mirror: Instant-return type with mirror lock-up device and special shock absorbers for minimum vibration.

Lens mount: Pentax bayonet-mount.

Film advance: Ratchet-type rapid-wind lever. 20-degree pre-advance and 160-degree advance angle. "Cocked" indicator alongside shutter release button.

Exposure counter: Automatic reset.

Film rewind: Rapid-rewind crank for speedy film take-up.

Flash synchronization: X contact hot-shoe for cordless flash connection. FP + X contacts for conventional flash cord connection. X synchronization at 1/60 sec.

Exposure meter: Silicon-Photo-Diode meter measures central portion of ground glass at full aperture. Couples directly to shutter, aperture and film speed settings. Match needles for correct exposure. EV 1-18 for ASA 100 film with 50 mm lens. Film speed from 8 to 6400 ASA. Powered by two 1.5-volt silver-oxide batteries.

Memo holder: Square metal sleeve for holding type/speed tab from top of film box.

Dimensions: With 50 mm f/1.4 lens: width 143 mm (5.6") × height 91.4 mm (3.6") × depth 94 mm (3.7").

Weight: 896 g (31.4 ozs.) with 50 mm f/1.4 lens. 631 g (22.1 ozs.) with no lens.

GENERAL CAMERA TECHNIQUES

Holding the Camera

Camera movement is one of the most common of all photographic problems. It is experienced by amateur and professional alike. It usually occurs when we are in a rush and careless about bracing the camera, or when we release the shutter improperly. If this happens while the film is being exposed, the end result is poor-quality prints or blurred, unsharp, negatives and transparencies. They leave a great deal to be desired when enlarged or projected. Extra care must be taken when using longer-focal-length lenses, because the greater magnification of these lenses also magnifies camera movement. Another factor to bear in mind is: the slower the shutter speed, the more care is needed to prevent camera movement. However, you can keep these problems to a minimum by practicing these techniques:

1. Hold the camera firmly, but avoid too rigid a grip which can create tension and result in movement.

2. After focusing, support the base of the camera and the lens in the palm of your left hand. Use the right hand for additional support and only the forefinger to press the shutter-release button.

3. Take a relaxed stance, with your feet spread. Brace your elbows against your body for additional support. If seated use the same bracing procedure.

4. Support yourself by propping yourself or the camera against something solid: a wall, car, railing, table, etc. Do this particularly when using shutter speeds longer than 1/125 sec.

5. *Always* press the shutter-release button *gently*.

Taking Care of Your Camera

Your Pentax camera is a sophisticated, precision instrument built to give long-lasting, reliable, service. It will serve you well if you treat it right, with proper handling and reasonable care. The major causes of damage are:

Keep your camera ready for unexpected horseplay when around children and you won't miss good shots that only last for a split second. A winder or motor drive can also come in handy in such situations.

1. Dropping or banging the camera against immovable objects, which can damage the camera in many ways.

2. Water damage, particularly if the camera is submerged in salt water. *Cameras are not waterproof!* They must be protected from salt spray at the beach, splashing of any kind, and shielded from the rain. If your camera does get soaked, wipe it dry immediately and rush it to a Pentax service center. When you are shooting around water, take a large plastic bag and cut a hole for the lens. Place the camera in the bag with the tip of the lens extending through the hole, and use a rubber band to hold the plastic in place. Seal the open end of the bag, you will still be able to operate the controls and keep the camera protected from the elements.

3. Dirt and sand can cause serious damage to the shutter and other moving parts of the camera. Plastic bags are good protection when working where these conditions exist, both for storing and while shooting.

4. Humidity and temperature extremes should be avoided. Keep your camera out of direct sunlight, car trunks, and glove compartments. Shooting outdoors in winter presents a problem since batteries won't function if they get too cold. In cold weather carry your camera under your coat or jacket to keep the batteries warm. If the lens fogs up when you take the camera out to shoot, it will clear up in a short time.

5. Vibration experienced when you are traveling in a car, plane, or ship, can cause screws to loosen. To minimize this problem use foam-rubber padding about one inch thick to line the bottom of your camera bag. On longer trips I also use 1/4 inch foam rubber wrapped around my cameras and lenses individually, before packing them in my shoulder bag.

6. Amateur repairmen are a serious menace

PENTAX K-SERIES COMPARISON CHART

Features	K2	K2DMD	KX	KM	K1000
Shutter	5-Bladed Metal Electronic	same as K2	Rubberized-Silk Curtain	same as KX	same as KX
Flash Synchronization	X Hot-Shoe FP & X Contacts 1/125 sec.	same as K2	X Hot-Shoe FP & X contacts 1/60 sec.	same as KX	X Hot-Shoe X contact 1/60 sec.
Through-the-Lens Exposure Metering	Needle Matching Center Wtd.	same as K2	same as K2	Needle Centering Full-Frame Averaging	same as KM
Fully-Automatic Exposure	Yes	Yes	No	No	No
Shutter Speeds	8 sec. to 1/1000 sec.	same as K2	1 sec. to 1/1000 sec.	same as KX	same as KX
Shutter-Button Lock	Yes	Yes	Yes	No	No
Exposure Measurement Element	Silicone Photo Diode	same as K2	same as K2	Cadmium Sulfide	Cadmium Sulfide
Battery Check	Light Emitting Diode	same as K2	Meter Needle	same as KX	same as KX
Aperture Shown In Viewfinder	No	Yes	Yes	No	No
Mirror Lock-Up	Yes	Yes	Yes	No	No
Motor Drive/Data Back Acceptance	No	Yes	No	No	No
Self-Timer	Yes	Yes	Yes	Yes	No
Depth-of-Field Preview Facility	Yes	Yes	Yes	Yes	No
Size (With 50 mm f/1.4 lens)	5.7″ × 3.6″ × 3.7″ (144 mm × 92 mm × 90.4 mm)	same as K2	5.6″ × 3.6″ × 3.7″ (143 mm × 91.4 mm × 94 mm)	same as KX	5.6″ × 3.6″ × 3.7″ (with 55 mm f/2) (143 mm × 91.4 mm × 83 mm)
Weight (Without lens)	24.2 oz. (680 g)	same as K2	22.1 oz (626 g)	21.8 oz. (887 g)	21.4 oz. (790 g)

Keep your equipment clean, and handle it carefully, for a lifetime of trouble-free use. One of the best cleaning aids is this combination camel's hair brush and blower. Keep it in your camera bag along with the other cleaning aids described in the text and use them regularly.

to today's sophisticated camera equipment. If a problem develops, do yourself a favor and take the camera to a professional repairman, preferably at an authorized Pentax service center. It will be less costly in the long run. Help the repairman find a solution to your problem by showing him examples of the flawed images, either negatives, prints, or transparencies.

Cleaning Your Equipment

Your camera and lenses need periodic cleaning to keep them operating properly. You need the following items to do the job right: Lens-cleaning fluid, lens-cleaning tissues (not the silicone-type used for eyeglasses), a bulb-type ear syringe, two soft, camel's-hair brushes (a small one for cleaning lenses only, and a larger brush about 1-1/2 wide for cleaning the camera body), Q-tips, and a clean, soft, handkerchief which has been laundered a few

times. Keep these handy in a small case in your camera bag.

Easy does it! Handle the body carefully and don't scrub the lenses. Clean the outside of the camera body and lenses first, using the larger brush, and then blow the dust out of hard-to-reach openings with the bulb syringe. Do the inside of the camera in the same way. *Never touch the mirror, shutter leaves, or curtain with your fingers!* Put a drop or two of lens-cleaning fluid on a Q-tip and clean the eyepiece. You can use a damp cloth to wipe the outside of the camera when it needs it. Use lens-cleaning fluid sparingly when cleaning lenses. Place a couple of drops on the lens-cleaning tissue, not directly on the lens itself. Wipe with a light, circular motion. Do this only when absolutely necessary.

If your camera is used infrequently; take it out at least every month or so and fire the shutter at each of its speeds. Operate all the camera controls to keep them moving freely.

## CHAPTER 3

The Pentax M Series

Following the success of the K-series cameras, Asahi introduced the Pentax MX and ME—the ultimate compact, fast-operating, precision 35 mm SLR cameras. The MX is billed as the world's smallest, lightest, full-featured, 35 mm SLR, while the ME is billed as the fully automatic 35 mm SLR it is. These models were a natural evolution for Asahi, and they started off an industry-wide trend to more compact 35 mm models.

The ME is the smaller of the two. Its camera body only weighs 17 oz., while the MX weighs only .5 oz. more (compared to the K2 which weighs 24.2 oz.). A new group of 24 SMC Pentax-M lenses were introduced for the MX and ME. Since the K- and M-series cameras have the same size bayonet lens-mount, this makes a total of 43 lenses to choose from. These range from fish-eyes and ultra-wide-angles through ultra-telephotos, as

Sunsets can be as effective in black and white as they are in color, but they can be quite tricky to meter for proper exposure. In this case I pointed the Pentax ME first at the sky, and then at the water, to see how much the exposure would vary. I then set the exposure-compensation dial between the two extremes and bracketed the resulting exposure.

The Pentax MX (left) and ME (right) are two of the world's smallest and lightest precision 35 mm single-lens reflex cameras. The Pentax MX is a full-control manual-exposure camera, and the ME is an automatic-exposure camera with exposure-compensation ability.

well as zooms, macros, and shift-control. You can also use older screw-mount Pentax lenses with a Mount Adapter B and stop-down metering.

Space-age electronics enabled Asahi's engineers to design these extremely small SLR cameras. Many of the larger moving parts were replaced with space-saving, solid-state, integrated circuits that do the job of a number of separate components. Connections made with flexible printed circuits are much more reliable than old-fashioned, failure-prone wiring. Where other systems rely on small cables, nylon cords, or gears and chains for mechanical coupling, these cameras use long-lasting, variable resistors to do the job electronically.

Moving parts which could not be replaced with electronics were made even larger and stronger than their counterparts. All of this advanced technology is housed in a tough die-cast body to make the MX and ME two of the most precise, dependable cameras ever made.

MX AND ME SIMILARITIES

The MX and ME are both 35 mm full-frame, SLR cameras with open aperture, center-weighted, through-the-lens metering. Since they have a number of features in common, we will look at these first and discuss their operating procedures.

Viewing and Focusing

The reflective surfaces of the pentaprism in both cameras have been silver coated, to provide brighter images in the viewfinder. This makes focusing easier, particularly in dim light. The MX and ME have the same deeply-recessed viewfinder which proved itself in the K-series cameras. If you wear glasses, diopter correction lenses which fit the eyepiece are available, from −3 to +2. A clip-on magnifier and a Refconverter (Right-angle finder) also fit the viewfinder eyepiece of both cameras.

The standard focusing screen provides three-way focusing. It has a small, split-image range-finder spot in the center, surrounded by a microprism collar, both set inside a ground-glass field. If you use a variety of lenses with your MX, there are seven additional focusing screens available to aid you in special situations. You can interchange these yourself, with a tweezer-like tool furnished with each accessory screen. The ME has a fixed screen only, but it's the most versatile one.

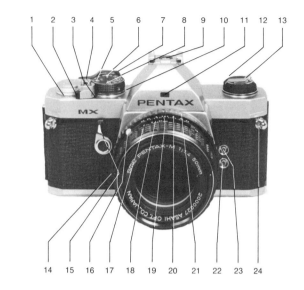

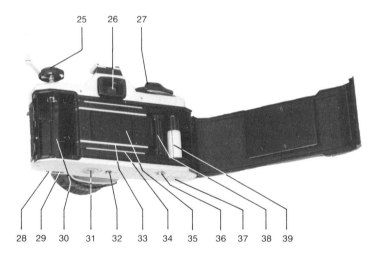

PENTAX MX—PARTS NOMENCLATURE

1. Frame counter
2. Shutter-button-lock lever
3. Shutter-cocked indicator
4. Shutter button
5. ASA-film-speed window
6. ASA-film-speed-dial lock button
7. Film-advance lever
8. Shutter-speed dial
9. Hot shoe
10. Shutter-speed index mark
11. Aperture-readout window
12. Film-rewind/back-cover-release knob

13. Film-rewind crank
14. Lens-release lever
15. Self-timer/depth-of-field-preview lever
16. Upraised lens-alignment dot
17. Focusing ring
18. Distance scale
19. Aperture/distance index mark
20. Depth-of-field scale
21. Aperture ring
22. X-sync terminal
23. FP-sync terminal
24. Neck-strap lug
25. Film-rewind/back-cover release knob

26. Viewfinder eyepiece
27. Film-advance lever
28. Winder-guide-pin channel
29. Winder-contact terminals
30. Film-cartridge chamber
31. Battery chamber
32. Tripod socket
33. Film rail
34. Film-guide rail
35. Shutter blades
36. Film-rewind button
37. Film-transport coupler
38. Film-sprocket spool
39. Film-takeup spool

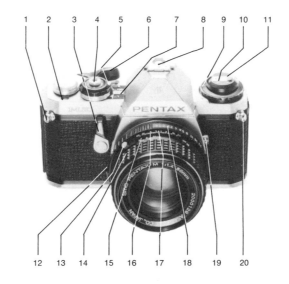

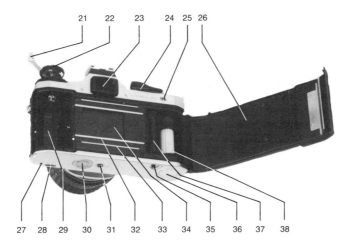

PENTAX ME—PARTS NOMENCLATURE

1. Neck-strap lug
2. Frame counter
3. Self-timer lever
4. Shutter-release button
5. Shutter-mode index mark
6. Film-advance lever
7. Shutter dial
8. Hot shoe
9. Exposure-compensation dial
10. Film-rewind/back-cover-release knob
11. Film-rewind crank
12. Lens-release lever
13. Upraised lens-alignment dot

14. Focusing ring
15. Distance scale
16. Depth-of-field scale
17. Aperture/distance index mark
18. Aperture ring
19. X-sync socket
20. Neck-strap lug
21. Film-rewind crank
22. Film-rewind/back-cover-release knob
23. Viewfinder eyepiece
24. Film-advance lever
25. Film-advance/rewind indicator

26. Film pressure plate
27. Winder-guide-pin channel
28. Winder-contact terminals
29. Film-cartridge chamber
30. Battery chamber
31. Tripod socket
32. Film rail
33. Film-guide rail
34. Shutter blades
35. Film-rewind button
36. Film-transport coupler
37. Film-sprocket spool
38. Film-takeup spool

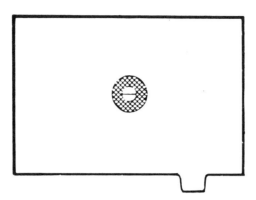

Both the MX and the ME have the same standard, three-way focusing screen (above). It consists of a central, split-image rangefinder, surrounded by a microprism ring set in a ground-glass field. This system has proven versatile under a variety of conditions. There are seven accessory screens available for the MX (below) which you can interchange yourself.

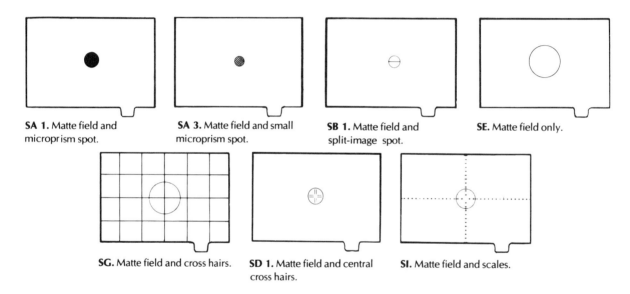

SA 1. Matte field and microprism spot.

SA 3. Matte field and small microprism spot.

SB 1. Matte field and split-image spot.

SE. Matte field only.

SG. Matte field and cross hairs.

SD 1. Matte field and central cross hairs.

SI. Matte field and scales.

To change the focusing screen in the MX, first remove the lens from the camera body. Then, using the small, tweezer-like tool that comes with the accessory screen, pull the screen-retainer pin in the camera toward you. The screen frame will then flip down. Again using the tool, grasp the screen by its little lip and remove it from the camera. Install the new screen by placing it on the screen frame and pushing the frame into its original position until it clicks. *Never* touch the screens with your fingers.

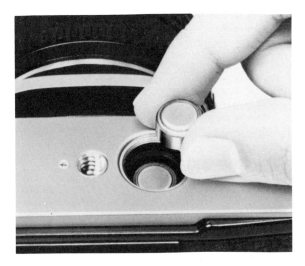

To insert batteries in either the Pentax MX or ME, first use a coin to remove the battery-chamber cover on the bottom of the camera. Then place the two 1.5-volt silver-oxide batteries in the battery chamber with the positive (+) side facing the chamber cover. Replace the chamber cover and you are ready to begin shooting.

Powering the Cameras

The Pentax MX and ME are powered by two 1.5-volt silver-oxide batteries. Installing the batteries should be done with the utmost care. Batteries can be damaged by acids in the skin, so handle them only by the edges with a clean, dry, cloth. Remove the battery-chamber cover by using a coin to unscrew it from the base of the camera. Turn the cover counterclockwise, in the direction of the arrow. Place the batteries (either Eveready S76E or Mallory MS76H) in with the positive (+) side up and replace the battery-chamber cover.

You can save battery power by getting in the habit of using the shutter-release lock which turns the power off. It stays off even when the lens cap is removed or the rapid-wind lever is extended away from the camera body. (These situations would normally turn the electrical system on.) When the lens cap is off, a slight, constant pressure on the shutter-release button will keep the power turned on. Your batteries could become depleted when you carry the cameras in a case where an object presses against the shutter-release button. Using the shutter-release lock will prevent this.

One set of batteries should last about a year with average use (approximately 10,000 shutter releases). Just to be safe, I replace mine every six months, and carry an extra set on extended trips. The LEDs in the viewfinder serve as a battery check each time you use the camera. When the batteries are weak, the lighted dot will flicker as a warning. If no dot lights up the batteries should be replaced immediately. When the batteries are drained, you can still operate the cameras under limited conditions. With the MX, which has a mechanically-operated shutter, only the meter will stop functioning. To keep shooting, simply estimate the exposure from past experience, or follow the exposure guide on the data sheet that came with the film you are using. The ME has just one mechanical shutter speed: 1/100 sec. If the batteries die, you must change to the 100X setting, estimate exposure, and use the proper aperture for that speed.

M-series meter and power switches function just as they do on K-series cameras.

Type: 35 mm full-frame SLR camera with open-aperture center-weighted through-the-lens metering.

Lens mount: Pentax K bayonet.

Standard lenses: SMC Pentax 50 mm f/1.2, SMC Pentax-M 50 mm f/1.4, SMC Pentax-M 50 mm f/1.7, SMC Pentax-M 40 mm f/2.8.

Shutter: Horizontal-run rubberized silk, focal-plane shutter; speeds from 1 to 1/1000 sec. plus B; shutter lock, and "cocked" indicator.

Flash synchronization: FP and X sockets, plus hot/cold accessory shoe for X contact; 1/60 sec. X synchronization.

Self-timer: Delays shutter release to 4—12 seconds; self-timer starter button provided.

Viewfinder: Silver-coated pentaprism finder; split-image microprism focusing screen (8 interchangeable screens); 95% of picture-taking area visible and 0.97X magnification with 50 mm lens at infinity); −0.5 diopter eyepiece. Information viewfinder shows f-stop, shutter speed and tri-colored LED read-out dots. Correction lens adaptor M, Magnifier M and Refconverter M fit the viewfinder frame.

Mirror and diaphragm: Instant-return mirror and automatic diaphragm. Depth-of-field preview with self-timer lever.

Film wind and rewind: Ratchet-type rapid-wind lever, plastic-tipped for winding comfort. 162-degree throw with a stand-off angle of 20 degrees. Rewind crank for speedy film rewind.

Film loading: Magic-needle loading.

Automatic winder: MX camera body accepts Winder MX for up to 2 frames-per-second (single-frame and consecutive exposure operation possible) and Motor Drive MX for up to 5 frames-per-second (single-frame and consecutive exposure operation possible), for automatic film wind and shutter cocking.

Exposure counter: Automatic-reset type.

Exposure meter: Open-aperture, center-weighted, through-the-lens meter, with GPD cells for fast light response, with tri-colored LED exposure read-out, rapid-wind lever and shutter release button acting as meter switch. Exposure range: EV1-19 (ASA 100, f/1.4), Film speed range: ASA 25-1600.

Power source: Two 1.5-volt silver-oxide batteries (G13); LED's double as battery-check lamp.

Back cover: Standard back with memo holder, interchangeable with Magazine Back MX and Dial Data MX.

Size: 135.5 mm (5.4 in.) × 82.5 mm (3.3 in.) × 49.5 mm. (1.9 in.)

Weight: 495 grams (17.6 oz.)

The Metering System

Gallium-Arsenide-Phosphide Photo Diodes (GPD) have been incorporated into the metering system of the MX and ME. These are space-age light sensors which measure the intensity of the light being transmitted through the camera lens. Asahi claims these new diodes respond 1,000 times faster than older CdS cells, which are still used in many cameras. This fast response eliminates any time lag in exposure measurement when you go from bright sunlight to a deep-shade situation, a problem with CdS meters. GPDs are insensitive to infrared rays and temperature extremes, which influence the more recently used silicon photo diodes.

Light-emitting diodes (LEDs) (in the MX and ME viewfinders) have replaced the bulkier, more vulnerable, match-needle meter-readout system. Since they have no moving parts, LEDs are shockproof, jamproof, and not affected by temperature or humidity extremes. The distracting flickering of lights experienced in some other LED systems was eliminated by using a new type of stabilizer circuitry. The only time two diodes light at the same time is when the meter calls for an exposure exactly between two settings.

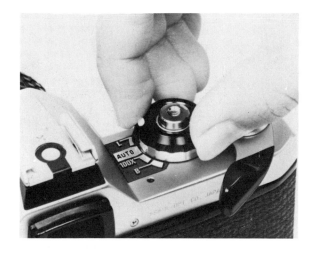

Setting the shutter dial of the Pentax ME to *L* (lock) prevents accidental firing of the shutter as well as accidental turning on of the electrical system, which will deplete the batteries.

PENTAX ME SPECIFICATIONS

Type: 35 mm full-frame SLR camera with aperture-preferred automatic exposure, electronic focal-plane shutter, and open-aperture center-weighted through-the-lens metering.

Lens mount: Pentax K bayonet.

Standard lenses: SMC Pentax 50 mm *f*/1.2, SMC Pentax-M 50 mm *f*/1.4, SMC Pentax-M 50 mm *f*/1.7, SMC Pentax-M 40 mm *f*/2.8, SMC Pentax 50 mm *f*/2.

Shutter: Seiko MFC vertical-run metal focal-plane shutter; automatic exposure electronically controlled between 8 and 1/1000 sec.; manual mechanical speed of 1/100 sec. plus B; provided with shutter button lock and "cocked" indicator.

Flash synchronization: X socket on front of camera body, plus X-contact hot/cold accessory shoe; X flash synchronizing at 1/100 sec.

Self-timer: Delays shutter release 4-12 seconds.

Viewfinder: Silver-coated pentaprism finder; split-image microprism focusing screen; 92% of picture-taking area visible and 0.97× magnification (with 50 mm lens at infinity); −0.5 diopter eyepiece. LED dots inside viewfinder indicate automatically selected shutter speeds, plus over- and under-exposure warning. Correction lens adaptor M, Magnifier M, and Refconverter M fit the viewfinder frame.

Mirror and diaphragm: Instant-return mirror and automatic diaphragm.

Film wind and rewind: Single-stroke rapid-wind lever, plastic-tipped for winding comfort. 135-degree throw with stand-off angle of 30 degrees. Rapid rewind crank for speedy film rewind.

Film loading: Magic-needle loading.

Automatic winder: ME camera body accepts the ME 1.5-frames-per-second automatic film winder, for consecutive or single frame exposure operation.

Exposure counter: Automatic-reset type.

Exposure meter: Open-aperture, center-weighted through-the-lens meter, with GPD cells for fast light response, with LED exposure read-out; rapid wind lever and shutter release button acting as meter switch. Exposure range; EV1-19 (ASA 100 *f*/1.4). Film speed range: ASA 12-1600. Exposure compensation dial: 1/4x, 1/2x, 1x, 2x, 4x.

Battery: Two 1.5-volt silver-oxide batteries (G13); LED's double as battery- check lamp.

Back cover: Standard back with memo holder, interchangeable with Dial Data ME for data recording on film.

Size: 131 mm (5.2 in.) × 82.5 mm (3.3 in.) × 49.5 mm (1.9 in.)

Weight: 460 grams (16.4 oz.)

The self-timer lever of the ME is on the left side of the front of the camera. It delays release of the shutter up to 12 seconds, depending how far down the lever is moved. The self-timer is activated by giving the lever a slight push upwards. Here the lever is shown in the cocked position.

Mirror Lock-up

Neither the MX nor the ME has a mirror lock-up feature. Instead, a specially-designed shock-absorbing, air damper cushions the rising mirror so efficiently, that Asahi claims a mirror lock-up system is unnecessary.

Self-Timer

The self-timer delays release of the shutter from 4 to 12 seconds, depending on how far you set the lever. The self-timer is also helpful when you want to make motion-free exposures with the camera on a tripod. If you wish, you can override the self-timer with the shutter-release button after the activating lever has been set. The self-timer can then be used for the next exposure or you can release it before advancing the film and cocking the shutter without exposing the film.

Flash Synchronization

There are two ways to synchronize electronic flash units with the MX or ME. The wireless hot shoe atop the pentaprism has a built-in X contact.

There is also a separate X-sync cord terminal located on the camera body. As with K-series cameras, the hot shoe becomes activated only after the electronic flash unit is mounted into the shoe. (This is a good safety feature which prevents electrical shock.) Electronic-flash-sync speeds on the MX range from 1/60 sec. down to B. Flash bulbs of the M, MF, or FP class can be used on X sync from 1/15 sec. down to B. FP-class flash bulbs can be synchronized with the MX from 1/60 to 1/1000 sec. by using the FP cord terminal. The ME has only one electronic sync speed: 1/100 sec. This faster speed helps keep ghost images to a minimum. For safety's sake, always keep the synchronization terminals covered, with the protective plugs provided, when not in use.

Multiple Exposures

Since there is no separate control for making multiple exposures, use the same method described for K-series cameras.

Film Loading and Unloading

M-series cameras have a "Magic Needle" take-up spool. Instead of the usual two or three slots found in most cameras, the "Magic Needle" take-up spool has 16 plastic rods. You push the tip of the film leader through any two of the rods, which grab and hold the film, even when it is inserted at an angle. Although light-leaking cartridges are rare today, it is still a good idea to load and unload your camera in a shady spot, or shield it from direct sunlight with your body. To load film, follow these six steps:

1. Open the camera back by lifting the crank of the rewind knob and pulling it upwards. If the camera is brand new, be sure to remove the plastic shield covering the pressure plate. (This is only used for protection during shipping.)

2. Slide the film cartridge into the film chamber with the flat side up. Lock the cartridge in place by pushing the rewind knob down, rotating it slightly making sure that it grips the spool.

3. Pull the film leader extending from the cartridge out far enough to reach the take-up spool. Now insert the end between any of the 16 semi-flexible plastic rods of the "Magic Needle" take-up spool. There is no need to hunt for a specific slot.

4. Advance the film slowly, until the perforations on both sides of the film engage the sprocket teeth.

5. Close the camera back, making sure that it snaps firmly into place.

6. As an added precaution, take up any slack left in the film by turning the rewind crank clockwise until the film feels taut. Do not force it! Now advance the film slowly with the rapid-wind lever and make sure that the film-rewind knob is turning counterclockwise. If it does, you know that the film has been loaded properly. Continue advancing the film and releasing the shutter until the exposure-counter window shows the first dot between 0 and 2 in the center. This is frame #1, and now you are ready to start shooting.

On the ME, there is another way to check if the film is moving through the camera properly. There is a film-advance indicator in a small win-

The backs of both the Pentax MX and ME open by pulling the film-rewind knob upwards. Sometimes it is easier to first lift the film-rewind crank out of the knob and pull the crank up.

After opening the camera back and putting the film cartridge in the film chamber on the left, simply insert the end of the film leader between any two rods of the take-up spool. It is a good idea to then advance the film a few frames and make sure the perforations on both sides of the film engage the sprocket teeth properly.

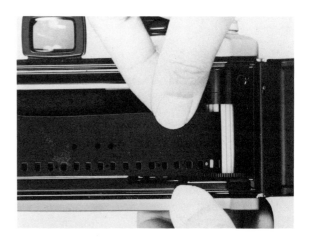

Use a fast shutter speed when shooting photographs of action. Splashing, jumping, and diving call for a speed around 1/500 sec.

dow located on the upper-right side of the camera back. Two vertical red lines appear when there is no film in the camera. A single red vertical line tells you that film is loaded and advanced. As you advance the film, a flickering red image appears to indicate it is moving properly.

Both the MX and ME have another unique feature, the shutter-cocked indicator. This is a tiny window opening on top of the camera near the rapid-wind lever. It turns red when the shutter is fully cocked, and goes dark after the shutter is released. This is a great help in avoiding embarrass-

ing moments, when you press the shutter and nothing happens because you forgot to advance the film and cock the shutter. Also, get into the habit of checking the shutter-cocked indicator before putting your camera away. Release the shutter if it is cocked, so that the delicate springs will not be kept under tension when the camera isn't being used.

When you reach the end of the roll, the rapid-wind lever will stop moving rather abruptly. This often happens at some point in the middle of a stroke. The shutter-release button also locks at this point. Resist the urge to force the lever further, or you can damage the film, camera, or possibly both. Instead, lift the rewind knob to its rewind position, press the rewind button (which is recessed in the base of the camera) and wind the knob clockwise. Wind it slowly to avoid getting static electricity marks on the film.

You will feel a slight snap when the film leader releases from the take-up spool. Continue winding, until you are sure the film leader is inside of the cassette. (This will help you avoid double exposing an already exposed roll accidentally. If the film leader is gone there is no question that the roll has been exposed.) Another precautionary measure I take is to always try to rewind the film as soon as I have made the last exposure. It is easy to forget there is film in the camera, and you open the back by accident, producing light-struck, ruined negatives or transparencies.

Switching Film

Have you ever wanted to change from one type of film to another after shooting just part of a roll? There is a simple way to do this. First note the frame number where you stopped, and mark it on the film container. (I carry a sheet of self-adhesive labels for this purpose.) Now, repeat the rewind process as described above, but with one exception. *Stop rewinding as soon as you feel and hear the film leader release from the take-up spool.* This will leave the film leader extending outside of the cartridge, so that you can reload again when you want to finish up the roll. At that time, load in the usual way. With the lens cap covering the lens, continue to advance the film and release the shutter until you have reached the number past the one noted when the film was removed. This should prevent overlapping of images.

Setting Film Speed

The ASA film-speed window is in different positions on the MX and ME. On the MX you will find it on top of the shutter-speed dial, along with a small, round metal ASA dial-lock button. It has settings for films with ASA ratings from 25 to 1600. (The ASA speed appears at the top of the film information sheet which comes with the film, and is usually marked on the film box and cartridge as well.)

To change the setting, first pull the rapid-wind lever away from the body, for easier manipulation. Press the dial-lock button and hold it down while turning the outer ring of the shutter-speed dial. Turn the dial until the correct ASA number appears

To set the ASA film speed on the Pentax MX, press the dial-lock button on the top of the shutter-speed dial and turn the outer ring of the dial. Turn this ring until the desired film speed aligns with the red dot above the small window on the dial.

The ASA film-speed dial of the Pentax ME is around the base of the film-rewind knob. To set the film speed, lift the ring on the very outer edge, and turn it until the proper ASA number aligns with the orange index mark.

The lens mounting and removal procedure is same for all Pentax M-series and K-series cameras. To mount lenses, align the red dot on the front of the camera with the red dot on the lens. Insert the lens and turn it clockwise until it locks into place. (In dim light you can align the raised white dot on the lens with the lens-release lever on the camera body.)

To remove a lens, press the lens-release lever (on the lower left of the camera's lens-mounting flange) and turn the lens counterclockwise until you can lift it out.

next to the red dot on the dial. There are click-locks which operate when you release the lock button, so make sure the dial locks into the setting you've chosen. This is very important, since the film-speed setting programs the exposure meter for the exposure requirements of that particular film.

On the ME, lift the ring on the outer edge of the film-rewind dial base, and turn the ring until the proper ASA number reaches the orange index mark. When you lower the ring it locks into place.

Lens Mounting and Removal

To mount a lens, first remove the camera-body cap and the rear-lens cap. Holding the camera body in your left hand and the lens in your right, align the red dot on the camera's lens-mounting-ring with the red dot on the edge of the lens flange. Insert the lens carefully into the body, and turn clockwise until it snaps into place. (Most SMC Pentax M lenses have a raised white align-ment dot on the lens barrel for use in low-light-level situations. By resting your left thumb on the lens-release lever and your right thumb on the raised dot, and then lining up the two thumbs, the lens is in the proper place for insertion.)

To remove a lens, hold the camera body in

your left hand and press the lens-release lever down with your thumb. Now turn the lens coun-terclockwise with your right hand until it stops. Then remove the lens from the body.

If you have to put a lens down without the rear lens cap, place it with the front element down,

If you should have to put a lens down without the rear lens cap on, place it with the front down to avoid damaging the lens-coupling mechanism.

to avoid damaging the lens coupling mechanism. Always replace the camera-body cap if you are storing lenses separately, to prevent lint and dust from getting into the mirror and shutter mechanisms.

Lens-Aperture Ring

To control the amount of light coming through the lens, each lens has an internal diaphragm with an adjustable aperture. You regulate the size of the aperture opening by turning the lens-aperture ring. There are a series of numbers marked on the aperture ring which indicate f-stops. F-stops are equivalent to the amount of light admitted by the lens at each opening. (They have been calibrated from the ratio between the diameter of the lens opening to the focal length of the lens.) The f-stop with the highest number has the smallest opening, conversely the f-stop with the lowest number has the widest opening. Most lens-aperture rings have click stops at each f-stop and also half way between them, to indicate 1/2 stop adjustments. Each succeeding higher f-stop (for example, a change from f/2 to f/4) cuts the amount of light reaching the film in half. Each lower f-stop doubles the amount of light.

Depth of Field

Depth of field is the area of acceptable sharpness in front of and behind the point of focus. This varies with the size of the lens aperture. The depth of field becomes progressively greater as the lens opening becomes smaller. The distance at which the lens is focused also affects the depth of field: it increases as you get further away. Another factor which determines depth of field is the focal length of the lens. The shorter the lens, the greater the depth of field. As the focal length increases, the depth of field narrows (at the same aperture and camera-to-subject distance).

Open-aperture viewing is most convenient for composing and focusing, but shows the least amount of depth of field since the widest lens opening is being used. It is important to check your depth of field with the lens stopped down to the picture-taking aperture, particularly when using the wider apertures.

There are two ways to determine the depth of

Since the Pentax ME does not have a depth-of-field previewing feature you must use the depth-of-field scale on the lens instead. This lens is set at f/4 and focused at 15 ft. The depth-of-field scale shows a range of sharpness extending from about 13 ft. to 20 ft.

field on the Pentax MX. It can be checked visually in the viewfinder, using the depth-of-field-preview lever, or you can use the depth-of-field scale in front of the aperture ring on the lens. The depth-of-field-preview lever on the MX is the same lever used to set the self-timer. When you move the lever towards the lens mount the lens stops down to the picture-taking aperture. The lens returns to the widest aperture when the lever is released.

The Pentax ME does not have a depth-of-field-preview lever, but you can use the depth-of-field scale instead. First focus the camera, then move the aperture ring to the picture-taking aperture. Now check the f-stop numbers on the scale in front of the aperture ring. Notice the alignment in relation to the distance markings on the focusing-ring scale. Your depth of field is between the distances aligned with the proper pair of f-stop numbers.

Stop-Down Metering

Open-aperture, fully-automatic, lenses stay open at their widest aperture to make focusing and composing easier. However, older non-automatic, screw-mount, Takumar lenses, the SMC ultra-tele-photos, and most extension tubes and bellows for close-up photography, *do not have meter coupling* and must be used with stop-down metering. You

47

The concept of depth-of-field is demonstrated here using two pieces of driftwood placed 12 in. apart. A 50 mm lens was used for all the photographs.

In the photograph above the lens was opened to the maximum aperture, and focused on the piece on the left. The piece in the back is obviously out of focus.

In the above right photograph the same maximum aperture was used, but this time the lens was focused on the rear piece, and the forward one is obviously out of focus.

In the photograph on the right the lens was stopped down to f/16 and focused approximately 1/3 of the distance behind the foward piece of driftwood. As you can see, this combination of small aperture and careful positioning of focus makes both pieces appear sharp and clear.

The self-timer lever of the MX (below) plays a dual role, for it is also the depth-of-field preview control. Pushing the lever towards the lens stops the lens down to the picture-taking aperture, giving a visual indication of the depth of field.

do this by moving the aperture ring to the f-stop you wish to use in order to take a meter reading. The meter will then give you the shutter speed required for that opening.

Since it is easier to compose and focus at the widest lens opening, you should do so before stopping down the aperture to take a reading and make the exposure. The viewing screen becomes progressively dimmer as you turn the aperture ring. While the Pentax Auto-Extension Tube Set K allows you to use open-aperture metering, the other K-series accessories which do require stop-down metering are as follow: Standard Extension Tube Set K, Helicoid Extension Tube K, Auto Bellow K and Bellow Unit K.

Infrared Focusing

If you decide to try infrared black-and-white film, you must use the following focusing proce-

Both the MX and ME have accessory backs with which you can change them to data-imprinting cameras. The MX can be used with either the Pentax Data MX back or the Pentax Dial Data MX back, both of which are shown here.

dure. First take a look at the depth-of-field scale on the lens. You will see a small orange line to the left of the central diamond-shaped mark. (On some lenses this is a small red R.) This is the infrared focusing mark. Focus the camera as you would normally, but move the distance figure at the center mark to the infrared mark before making your exposures. This is necessary because infrared rays focus at a different film plane than visible rays of light. It is not true for infrared color film, which can be used in the normal manner.

Data Backs

The standard back of the MX and ME is simple to remove and replace with the Dial Data MX or Dial Data ME back. These backs convert the cameras into data-imprinting cameras. With them you can record the year, month, and day, or technical data such as the aperture, shutter speed, and frame number right on the film frame.

In addition, the letters from A to M can be added to the numerals from 0 to 36, and your choice of data will be imprinted automatically, in a corner of the film. The MX also accepts the 250-exposure Magazine Back MX.

Tripod Mounting

Don't mount your MX or ME on any tripod, until you've measured how far the tripod screw extends above the base plate. If it is longer than 3/16, the depth of the socket, the screw could puncture the bottom of the socket, penetrating and damaging the inner workings of the camera. To prevent this, each camera is furnished with a plastic spacer ring, 2 round and just under 1/8 thick, with a hole in the center. You should place it between the tripod baseplate and the camera base. The spacer ring also makes it easier to mount the camera when using large-diameter lenses.

The Pentax MX and ME come supplied with a plastic spacer ring. This ring should be used with all tripods which have mounting screws longer than 3/16 in., otherwise the screw may penetrate and damage the camera body.

There are two major differences between the cameras. The MX is manually operated, while the ME has fully-automatic exposure operation with exposure compensation ability. They also have different types of shutters. The MX has a mechanical, horizontal-run, focal-plane shutter of rubberized silk. The ME has a Seiko MFC vertical-run, focal-plane, metal shutter, electronically controlled with stepless speeds. We will now examine how these differences relate to operating the cameras.

Controlling Exposure

The basic function of your camera controls is to deliver the correct amount of light to the film in the camera and give you the best rendering of your subjects. Two controls work together to achieve this: the lens-aperture ring and the shutter-speed dial. There is a third control on the ME: the exposure-compensation dial. We've examined the lens-aperture ring previously. Now we will take a look at the operation of the shutter-speed dial and the exposure-compensation dial.

MX Shutter-Speed Dial

Operating the shutter-speed dial is easier if you move the rapid-wind lever out from the camera body. The MX has 12 markings on the top of the dial: *B, 1, 2, 4, 8, 15, 30, 60✕ , 125, 250, 500, 1000,* with click-stops at each setting. You turn the dial either clockwise or counterclockwise to the speed you wish to use. The number *1* stands for 1 sec., after which each number represents fractions of a second. The number *2* represents 1/2 sec., *4* represents 1/4 sec., *8* represents 1/8 sec., etc., all of the way up to 1/1000 sec. *60✕* is marked in red to remind you that this is the highest speed you can use for synchronization with electronic flash units. For time exposures longer than 1 sec. you must use *B* (bulb). At this setting the shutter stays open as long as the shutter-release button is held down. It closes when the shutter button is released. If you are shooting extremely-long exposures, such as for a moonlit scene, and do not have a cable release

with a locking device, the shutter lock can be used to achieve the same result. Depress the shutter-release button and, as you hold it down, gently move the shutter lock into place. To close the shutter, keep the shutter-release button depressed while gently unlocking the shutter lock, then gradually release the shutter-release button, so as not to jar the camera.

ME Shutter Dial

Since there are only four settings, Asahi has shortened the name of the ME's shutter-speed dial to "shutter dial".

B (bulb) is used for time exposures *longer* than the 8 second capability of the automatic shutter. On this setting, the shutter remains open as long as you press the shutter-release button, and closes when the shutter button is released. For crisp, sharp, pictures, I use a cable release with a locking device to avoid jarring the camera during long exposures.

100✕ must be used for electronic-flash synchronization both when the flash unit is mounted in the hot shoe, or connected with a PC cord plugged into the camera's X-sync terminal. Another use for the *100✕* setting is in an emergency, when the batteries are drained and replacements are not available. The automatic features, including the meter and the electronic shutter, stop working when the batteries are exhausted. Since the *100✕* (or 1/100 sec.) is a mechanical shutter speed, it is not dependent on battery power. If there is enough light for a 1/100 sec. exposure, you can set the lens-aperture ring to the proper f-stop and continue shooting. With the meter inoperative, you will have to estimate the aperture setting to use. (The data sheet that comes with the film can help as a guide.)

AUTO is the setting used regularly with this fully-automatic camera, so Asahi designed the white index button to also serve as a shutter-dial lock, when the camera is set on *AUTO*. This is to help prevent your moving the dial off of *AUTO* accidentally.

This photograph was shot with the Pentax ME using a 200 mm lens and a shutter speed of 1/1000 sec. The camera was set on *Automatic*, and no exposure compensation used, because I wanted to silhouette the water skier against the bright, hazy background.

This MX shutter-speed dial is set on *B*, which stands for bulb, and means that the shutter will stay open as long as the shutter-release button is depressed.

This is the ME shutter dial. It is set on *Auto,* meaning automatic exposure.

L (Lock) prevents your firing the shutter accidentally. It is particularly useful when carrying the camera with a motor drive, or winder, attached and ready to be used. If the motor drive is set in the sequential mode even slight pressure can use up a number of exposures.

MX Viewfinder Display

The shutter-speed read-out is located on the right side of the MX's viewfinder. The speeds appear on a clear, semicircular disc which rotates as you turn the shutter-speed dial. Three shutter speeds are visible at a time. The speed you have chosen is in the center, the next-fastest speed is seen above the center and the next-slowest speed is below. An aperture-read-out window is located just above the viewing screen. The *f*-stops are read directly from the aperture ring, through a window in front of the pentaprism.

The exposure read-out panel is a series of five vertical LEDs on the right side of the viewfinder. These have a traffic-light sequence. The center LED turns green when the exposure you select is correct. If you need a half-stop less or a half-stop more exposure, the proper LED either above or

below the center turns yellow. When either of the LEDs at the top or bottom turn red, it is to alert you that the exposure is one or more stops under or over proper exposure, depending on the position of the light. Overexposure is indicated by the top LED, and underexposure is indicated by bottom LED.

The viewfinder of the Pentax MX shows the selected aperture (*f*-stop) above the center of the viewing screen. Three shutter speeds are shown on a moving circle at the right. The center shutter speed is the one set, and the other two are the next faster and next slower speeds. The five LED's on the right are the meter read-out.

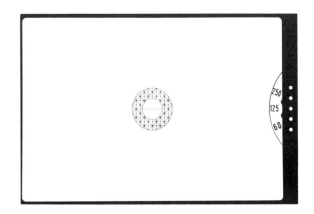

ME Viewfinder Display

The ME's shutter-speed read-out is located on the left side of the viewfinder, rising vertically from the bottom. There are 14 shutter speeds from 8 seconds to 1/1000 sec. with the words *Over* at the top and *Under* at the bottom. A set of 16 LEDs adjoin these. When you turn the meter on, one of the LEDs will light up indicating whether the conditions are over, under, or if there is enough light for a correct exposure. If there is enough light for proper exposure, an LED will light up next to the approximate shutter speed selected by the camera's meter. Approximate shutter speed you ask? Yes, because the electronic shutter of the ME has a stepless range of speeds. If the meter calls for 1/240 sec. the camera will shoot at 1/240 sec. and the closest LED at 1/250 sec. will light up. If you wish to use a slower or faster shutter speed, you can do so by changing the aperture setting of the lens.

ME Viewfinder Cap

Keep the small, plastic viewfinder cap that comes with the ME in your camera bag. You will need it when the camera is being used on a tripod, in the Auto mode, and your eye is away from the viewfinder. This cap slides over the eyepiece, preventing stray light from entering the viewfinder and reaching the meter, which could cause exposure errors.

ME Exposure-Compensation Dial

The exposure-compensation dial plays an important part in the exposure-control system of the ME, because there are no mechanical shutter speeds except *100×* and *B.* The exposure-compensation control is housed in the revolving base of the film-rewind knob. There are 5 click-stop settings marked on the dial: 4× , 2× , 1× , 1/2× , 1/4× . *1×* is used for normal automatic exposures and has white figures. All of the other settings are marked in red to remind you to return the dial to *1×* . Each setting changes the exposure by its factor. The *4×* setting adds two stops more exposure.

Five LED's visible on the right side of the Pentax MX viewfinder constitute the exposure-meter read-out. When the center (green) diode is lit correct exposure is indicated. The orange LED's in either direction indicate one-half stop under- or overexposure. The red LED's at top and bottom indicate a full stop or more variation from normal exposure.

For example: when the meter calls for 1/125 sec. at *f*/16 and the dial is set at *4×*, your exposure will become 1/30 sec. at *f*/16. The *2×* setting adds one stop more, the *1/2×* subtracts one stop and *1/4×* subtracts two stops exposure. Although there are

The exposure-compensation dial of the Pentax ME is located on the ring around the base of the film-rewind knob. The normal setting for this dial is *1X.* The other settings provide one or two stops more or less exposure.

no intermediate click-stops between these settings, the exposure-compensation control will work to give you intermediate settings when the dial is placed between click-stops.

The center-weighted, automatic-exposure system of the Pentax ME produces consistent results under a wide range of picture situations. It works best when taking pictures of an average scene. What is an average scene? One definition I like is: An evenly-lighted subject which has a me-dium range of contrast, photographed in a setting of average brightness. An example might be a city street scene with a small portion of sky, tall buildings, people in the foreground, and the sun behind you. All balancing out as an average scene.

Let's take the same scene at sunset. Now the massive buildings are back-lighted, casting deep shadows in front of them. The mood suggests dramatic silhouettes against the sky. To capture this effect expose for the sky, by adjusting the expo-

In order to show detail in the street in front of these buildings I knew I needed a stop less exposure than average. To get this exposure with the Pentax ME set on *Automatic,* I used the exposure-compensation dial on the $1/2 \times$ setting.

The shadows in this silhouette help make the beach scene more interesting. Place your hand over the foreground and you will see what I mean.

sure-compensation dial to the *1/4×* mark. (Reducing the "average scene" exposure by two stops.) If you would rather have details visible in the buildings and foreground, the reverse would be true. You would set the exposure-compensation dial to *4×* or *2×* to increase the exposure by two or one stops over the automatic-exposure reading.

The exposure-compensation dial is handy for all back-lighted scenes, including portraits. Side-lighting may only call for an exposure increase of 1/2 to a full stop. When in doubt about proper exposure, do what the pros do. Try a number of exposures with 1/2 stop differences. This is called "bracketing."

When photographing brightly-lit subjects against large dark backgrounds, such as perform-ers at an ice show, use the exposure-compensation dial to stop down one to two stops. This is because the meter will be influenced by the dark background. Remember to experiment to see what works for you with your equipment.

Remember that the camera meter cannot do your thinking for you. Don't allow yourself to get trapped into making only automatic exposures all of the time or you will have many disappointments, particularly with color film (which does not have the latitude that black-and-white film has). You must decide when to override the camera meter's "average scene" reading with the exposure-compensation dial, to render the mood or feeling you want.

THE MV

The Pentax MV was introduced in the fall of 1979. At first glance the MV appears to be a stripped-down version of the fully-automatic ME. A closer look will reveal that Asahi has retained the major features of the ME and eliminated a few of the minor ones. However, they have also added some new features and have reduced its weight by 1.4 oz.

The Pentax MV is the ideal camera for the person who would like to be able to just "aim and shoot". The photographer who wants a fully-automatic 35 mm SLR that is easily operated, and also requires the least amount of financial investment. Built with the same high-quality construction as all Asahi cameras, the MV can be used with all Pentax SMC bayonet-mount lenses, and many Pentax accessories.

The Pentax MV is a small, light, inexpensive, fully automatic 35 mm SLR.

ME—MV DIFFERENCES

MV Viewfinder Display

A major change is the new, "Stop and Go" metering-information system in the MV. This replaces the ME's LED shutter-speed-indication system on the left side in the viewfinder. When the system is activated by pressing the shutter release part way, three oval-shaped diodes one above the other light up individually, either red, green, or yellow. You use these to take an exposure reading. When you see the:

Green Light—This means "A OK! Fire Away." Trip the shutter and the correct exposure will be made for the *f*-stop you have chosen. It will be made at a stepless shutter speed ranging from *over* 1/30 sec. up to 1/1000 sec.

Red Light—This means "Overexposure". Change the aperture setting to a smaller opening. Do this until the green light comes on.

Yellow Light—This is the slow-shutter-speed warning. A shutter speed of 1/30 sec. *or slower* will be used by the camera at this aperture. Be

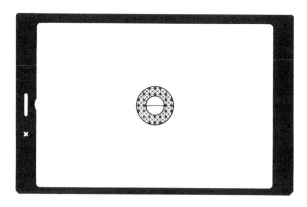

This is the viewfinder of the Pentax MV. The three LED's which constitute the metering-information system appear in the narrow white area to the left of the viewing screen. The "X" shaped LED just below this area is the flash-ready indicator which lights up when a Pentax AF 200S flash is mounted on the camera and ready to fire.

careful, since such a slow shutter speed produces a chance of camera movement when handholding the camera. Try a wider aperture setting. If this doesn't change the light to green, either brace the camera firmly, place it on a tripod, or switch to flash.

This metering system uses a fast-reacting SPD (silicon photo diode) cell light-sensor instead of the gallium photo diodes used in the ME.

Another new feature in the viewfinder of the MV is the *X*-shaped diode-lighted signal, located just below the "Stop and Go" diodes. This is the MV's flash-ready indicator. It becomes operational *only* when the new Pentax AF 200S dedicated electronic flash unit is used, in the camera's *Auto* mode. It lights up when the flash unit is fully recycled and ready to be fired. (See Flash chapter for the AF 200S specifications.)

The MV has an aluminum-coated pentaprism instead of the silver coating used in the ME to enhance the brightness of the image in the viewfinder, with little loss of brilliance.

PENTAX MV SPECIFICATIONS

Type: 35 mm full-frame SLR camera with aperture-preferred automatic exposure, auto flash synch (with AF 200 S Auto Flash).

Mount: Pentax Bayonet Mount

Standard lenses: SMC Pentax-M 50 mm *f*/2, SMC Pentax 50 mm *f*/1.2, SMC Pentax-M 50 mm *f*/1.4, SMC Pentax-M 50 mm *f*/1.7, SMC Pentax-M 40 mm *f*/2.8.

Shutter: Seiko MFC vertical-run, metal, focal-plane shutter; shutter speeds automatically varied between 1 sec. and 1/1000 sec.; mechanical settings of "100 X" and "B" provided (operates without batteries at manual settings).

Exposure metering: Open-aperture, center-weighted, through-the-lens exposure metering via SPD cell. Exposure range from EV 3 (ASA 100 1/4 sec. at *f*/1.4, 1 sec. at *f*/2.8) to EV 19 (ASA 100 1/1000 sec. at *f*/22). Film Speed Range: ASA 25 to ASA 1600 (exposure compensation via ASA film speed dial. LED "Stop/Go" exposure readout in finder.)

Auto flash synch: Synchronizes automatically for AF 200S flash unit at 1/100 sec. via hot-shoe with shutter dial set to *Auto*; hot-shoe contact also provided for flash-ready indicator in viewfinder.

Manual flash synch: At "100X" (1/100 sec.) flash-synch setting of exposure mode dial (hot-shoe synch only).

Viewfinder: Aluminum-coated pentaprism finder with split-image/microprism focusing screen; shows 92% of the picture area, 0.85× magnification with 50 mm lens; −1.0 diopter eyepiece.

Viewfinder indications: Three LED Stop/Go indicator system. **Red:** overexposure; **Green:** Adequate exposure for handheld shooting (1/1000-1/30 sec.) **Yellow:** Slow Exposure Warning (below 1/30 sec., inadequate for handheld shooting) **"X":** AF 200 S flash-ready indicator.

Mirror and diaphragm: Instant-return mirror and automatic diaphragm.

Film wind and rewind: Single-stroke rapid-wind lever; plastic tipped for winding comfort, 135-degree advance with 30-degree rest setting. Rapid-rewind crank for speed film rewind.

Film loading: Magic-needle loading.

Exposure counter: Automatic reset, additive type.

Battery: Two 1.5-volt silver-oxide batteries; LEDs double as battery check lamp.

Back cover: Standard camera back with spring catch.

Size: 131 mm (5.2 in.) × 82.5 mm (3.3 in.) × 49.5 mm (1.9 in.)

Weight: 420 grams (14.8 ozs.)

Only cordless electronic flash units which can be synchronized via the hot-shoe on top of the pentaprism can be used with the MV. There are no separate PC terminals on the camera body.

Flash Synchronization

There are no camera-body PC terminals on the MV. Electronic flash units can be used only if they are the cordless type with hot-shoe synchronization. When one of these (or the AF 200S) is used on *manual,* the exposure-mode dial must be set to its *100X* setting. The AF 200S used with the camera on the *Auto* setting automatically synchronizes with the 1/100 sec. speed, and the flash-ready indicator in the viewfinder.

Exposure Compensation

There is no exposure-compensation dial on the MV, but the film-speed dial can be used for the same purpose. For example: If the ASA rating of the film you are using is 100, and you have a back-lighted subject, set the dial to 50 to add twice the exposure. When your subjects are spotlighted in front of dark backgrounds, double the ASA rating from 100 to 200 to decrease the exposure by 2X. There is an exposure-compensation-indicator dial located under the film-rewind crank to use as a guide in making adjustments.

Other Differences

The features eliminated by Asahi's designers are: camera-back memo holder, shutter lock, film-advance/rewind indicator. Also, this camera cannot be used with a motor drive or auto winder.

THE MV–1

This camera is a "Special Edition" version of the MV described previously. It was placed on the market in the early part of 1980. Retaining the same basic design as the original MV, Asahi has added the following features to give the camera greater versatility:

1. Auto winder acceptance (ME OR ME II).
2. Self-timer (4 to 10 sec. delay).
3. Interchangeable back.
4. Film-memo holder.

The MV–1 is slightly smaller than the MV, with a .2 oz. increase in weight. Operating procedures are the same. It is still economically priced for a fully-automatic camera with its capability.

The Pentax MV-1 is a special edition of the older MV with some additional features.

THE ME SUPER

In the true Pentax tradition, Asahi has again come up with another novel feature: push-button, electronic control of manual shutter speeds. This innovation, and other changes, make the "SUPER" the trend-setter for automatic 35 mm SLR's with manual-override exposure control.

The ME SUPER is the newest of the Pentax M-series cameras. It is the first camera in the world to have push-button control of shutter speeds.

ME—ME SUPER DIFFERENCES

The ME SUPER was introduced in January of 1980. The major difference between the ME SUPER and ME cameras is the unique, electronic, push-button manual-exposure control system of the ME SUPER. Shutter speeds are set by an electronic-pulse, computerized, control system which also activates the three-color-coded, LED shutter-speed display inside the viewfinder. This feature eliminated the need for the shutter-speed dial used on most SLR cameras.

Electro-Pulse Manual Shutter-Speed Control

Set the "EP" manual control in motion by moving the exposure-mode dial to M. Press the shutter release part way and the system turns on. The green LED alongside the "M" in the viewfinder lights up and stays on, and either a green or yellow LED comes on beside one of the shutter-speeds. *Green*, if the shutter speed you select is 1/60 sec. or faster, *Yellow*, when the speed is 1/30 sec. or longer. This yellow light is a warning that you should either hold the camera very carefully, or should mount it on a tripod.

There are two push-buttons to the left of the exposure-mode dial that control the shutter speeds (instead of a conventional shutter-speed dial).

When you press the front button, the LED's move up the shutter-speed scale to the faster shutter speeds. When you press the rear button, the reverse happens. If the shutter speed you have chosen allows too much light, the red LED alongside the *OVER* mark at the top of the scale starts flickering. Conversely, if the chosen shutter speed admits too

The viewfinder display on the Pentax ME SUPER shows the full range of shutter speeds, as well as indicators for over- and underexposure, manual operation, flash readiness, and use of the exposure-compensation control.

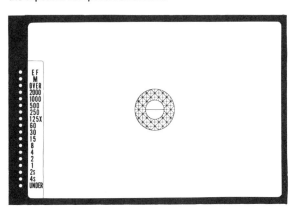

Type: 35 mm SLR camera with aperture-perferred automatic exposure; "pushbutton" electronic manual shutter speeds; auto flash synch (with AF 200S and AF 160 units).

Mount: Pentax bayonet mount with fully automatic diaphragm linkage.

Standard lenses: SMC Pentax 50 mm *f*/1.2, SMC Pentax-M 50 mm *f*/1.4, SMC Pentax-M 50 mm *f*/2, SMC Pentax-M 40 mm *f*/2.8, SMC Pentax-M 50 mm *f*/1.7.

Shutter: Seiko MFC-E2 vertical-run metal focal-plane shutter; automatic shutter speeds electronically controlled between 4 sec. and 1/2000 sec. (stepless variation), electronic manual shutter speeds at 14 viewfinder settings (controlled by dual pushbuttons), plus mechanical settings of "125X" and "B" (operates without batteries at mechanical settings); selection via exposure-mode dial; shutter-button lock also provided.

Auto flash synch: Synchronizes automatically with AF 200S or AF 160 flash units at 1/125 sec. via hot-shoe in both "AUTO" and "M" modes. LED flash synch/ready indication provided in viewfinder.

Manual flash synch: Direct X synch via hot-shoe or cord synch via X socket on camera body; 1/125 sec. flash synch speed at "125X" setting of exposure-mode dial.

Self-timer: Delays shutter release 4-10 seconds.

Exposure metering: Open aperture, center-weighted through-the-lens light metering by GPD cells. Exposure range from EV 1-EV 19 (ASA 100 with 50 mm *f*/1.4 lens). Film speed range: ASA 12-1600; 3-color LED shutter-speed readout in viewfinder.
(20-35 sec. display given on partially pressing shutter button which acts as metering switch.) ±2 EV exposure compensation via dial (1/4X, 1/2X, 2X, 4X).

Viewfinder: Silver-coated pentaprism finder with split-image/microprism focusing screen; shows 92% of the picture area, 0.95X magnification with 50 mm lens; −1.0 diopter eyepiece (accepts correction eyepieces).

Viewfinder indications: 2-color shutter speed readout: GREEN LEDs indicate speeds from 1/60 to 1/2000 sec. (adequate range for handheld shooting): YELLOW LEDs give camera shake warning for speeds from 4 sec. thru 1/30 sec.; RED LED "OVER/UNDER" exposure warning; RED LED exposure-compensation warning, "M" (manual) exposure warning when "M" LED is continuously lit, "M" auto flash ready indication when "M" LED flashes; auto flash synch indicated by GREEN LED at "125X."

Film loading: Magic-needle loading.

Film advance and rewind: Single-stroke, rapid wind lever, plastic-tipped for winding comfort. 135-degree throw with 30-degree standoff angle. Rewind via film-rewind crank. Couplings provided for use with 2 fps Winder ME II automatic film winder (also accepts Winder ME).

Exposure counter: Automatic reset type.

Batteries/battery check: Two 1.5-volt silver-oxide batteries power electronic systems in both AUTO and "M" exposure modes. LEDs in viewfinder flicker when batteries are low, cease to light on battery failure.

Back cover: Standard camera back with spring catch; removable for use of camera with Dial Date

Size: 131.5 × 83 × 49.5 mm (5.13 × 3.24 × 1.93 in.)

Weight: 445 grams (15.7 oz)

---

little light, the red LED beside the *UNDER* mark will start flickering. The flickering continues until you change one of the following: the shutter speed, the lens aperture, or the exposure-compensation dial. You have reached the correct exposure

setting when both the *OVER* and *UNDER* LEDs stop flickering.

I was quite skeptical when I first read about the new "electro-pulse" system. It sounded too much like an advertising gimmick. My doubts were allayed after I had used the ME SUPER for just a short time, and had experienced the convenience and speed of operation it offered. The ease of changing shutter speeds in manual mode without taking your eye away from the viewfinder is very functional. I found the system particularly useful for bracketing exposures, and when shooting fast-action subjects.

Viewfinder Display

There is an increase in brightness in the ME SUPER's viewfinder. This is a help in low-light-level and indoor shooting. Asahi used a new bright-matte focusing screen. It also makes focusing and reading the viewfinder-display scale much easier. The display scale now has speeds from 4 sec. to an increased top speed of 1/2000 sec. There is an additional *EF* symbol just above the *M*. This stands for "exposure-factor" and this LED starts flickering when you move the exposure-compensation dial. It continues flickering until you return the dial to the normal (*1x*) position. There is a battery-saving device which turns the metering system off automatically, after about 20 seconds, but it takes only slight pressure on the shutter-release button to turn it back on.

Flash Synchronization

There is a slight difference in the flash synchronization of the ME SUPER. This camera syncs at 1/125 sec. instead of 1/100 sec. This is also the only mechanical speed of the electronically-controlled vertical-run metal focal-plane shutter. It continues to operate without battery power, and can be used if your batteries become depleted.

Another feature is the "flash-ready/flash-synch indication" in the viewfinder. These indicators become operational when you mount one of the Pentax "dedicated" electronic flash units (see the descriptions of the AF 200s and the AF-160 in the chapter on flash photography). The LED beside the *125X* mark in the viewfinder lights up when a Pentax "dedicated" flash unit is mounted, to signal flash synch. When the flash unit is fully charged and ready to fire, the *M* LED starts to flicker. This system makes it unnecessary to check the ready-light on the flash unit.

Other Differences

The increased size of the air damper makes the ME SUPER the quietest Pentax camera yet, and one of the quietest SLR's on the market today. Its special cushioned mirror-return action assures vibration-free operation. In spite of the novel features of the ME SUPER, its body is slightly smaller, and weighs a half ounce less than the ME.

CHAPTER 4

The Pentax LX System

Asahi may have set a record when they introduced three 35 mm SLR cameras, three electronic flash units, and a variety of accessories in just one year: 1980. The first two cameras were simply improved versions of previous models, but the third one was a completely new concept for Asahi. This camera was the Pentax LX, and it was the first Pentax camera designed to meet the specific needs of professional and advanced amateur photographers. The product of over 60 years of experience, this camera took several years of development before being introduced in the American market in the second half of 1980.

(Editorial note. The material in this section was written before the LX was actually introduced. It was written from specification sheets and promotional material provided by the American headquarters of Pentax. In addition, Pentax provided the author with a prototype model of the LX for a short period of time, and assurances that this prototype was identical to the model which would be distributed in a few months.)

Asahi has continued their basic precept with the LX system: keeping the size and weight of the equipment to a minimum, without sacrificing performance or strength. Although it is slightly larger than the Pentax ME, the LX camera body weighs only four ounces more when equipped with the standard viewfinder. The best features of 35 mm camera design to date have been incorporated, along with several innovations. The result is a classic camera that is hard to beat.

THE LX CAMERA

The Pentax LX is a full-frame 35 mm single-lens reflex camera which offers a choice of aperture-preferred automatic exposure or manual exposure control. It uses a through-the-lens (TTL) "Integrated Direct Metering" (IDM) system which reads the light hitting the shutter curtain and film.

Viewing and Focusing

One of the major features of the Pentax LX system is the variety of its user-interchangeable viewfinders and focusing screens. There are six viewfinders available at this point in time: three eye-level finders, a "system" finder, and two waist-level finders. A unique feature of these viewfinders is that some have built-in, easily adjustable diopter correction of varying degrees. Two of the eye-level finders are adjustable from −1.5 to 0, the third from −3 to +1. The "Magni-finder's" range is from −5 to +4, and the "Magni-eyepiece" adjusts from −5 to +3. Another unique feature is that the "Action Eyepiece" viewfinder rotates a complete 180 degrees, giving you a viewing angle from eye-level to waist-level. If more space was avail-

The Pentax LX is a 35 mm SLR offering either aperture-preferred automatic exposure or fully manual exposure control.

able I could rhapsodize at length about this "Action Eyepiece". It is a "prayer come true" for photographers who wear glasses, for it allows you to see the entire frame without having to press your eyeball against the eyepiece, even when wearing diving goggles.

Changing viewfinders is a simple process. You press the finder-release lever, slide one finder off the camera, and replace it with another finder. Focusing screens are also easily changed. First remove the lens from the camera body, then remove the screen in the camera through the lens-mount opening with the tweezer-like tool furnished with each focusing screen. Install the new screen with the tweezer-like tool.

Viewfinder Display Automatic/Manual Operation

The full-information display inside the viewfinder of the LX tells you whether the camera is in automatic or manual mode, what aperture you are using, what shutter speed is set, whether the speed

selected by the camera is fast enough to permit hand holding the camera, if a dedicated Pentax flash is attached to the camera and ready to fire, and whether the camera is set for proper exposure. In addition there are warning symbols telling if the exposure-compensation dial is in use, if the shutter-speed dial is set to "B", or if the automatic-

Shown here is the Pentax LX camera body with the various finders and eyepieces available for the camera.

Type: 35 mm, full-frame, single-lens reflex camera, with IDM off-the-film-plane aperture-preferred automatic or full manual-exposure measurement, TTL integrated flash control with Pentax "T"-type flash units.

Lens Mount: Pentax bayonet mount with fully automatic diaphragm coupling.

Standard Lenses: SMC Pentax 50 mm f/1.2, SMC Pentax-M 50 mm f/1.4, 50 mm f/1.7, 50 mm f/2, 40 mm f/2.8.

Shutter: Electro-mechanical, horizontally-run, titanium focal-plane shutter; manual speeds mechanically controlled from 1/2000th sec. to "X" (1/75th sec.) and electronically controlled from 1/60th sec. to 4 seconds; mechanical speeds and "B" operational without batteries; automatic exposures electronically controlled in stepless range from 1/2000th sec. down to 125 seconds; shutter lock provided; shutter dial locks at "automatic" with push-button release; built-in curtain blind for use with Watch Data LX.

Flash Control: TTL measurement of ambient and electronic flash lighting directly off film plane with "T"-type Pentax flash models providing auto flash synch at "X" and visible ready light/exposure check in viewfinder when flash reaches full charge; automatic flash synch and visible viewfinder ready light with other Pentax dedicated flash models.

Flash Synchronization: FP terminal and X terminal, plus contacts for TTL integrated automatic flash control at camera front; FA-1 standard Finder features built-in X-synch hotshoe with TTL contacts.

Self-Timer/Preview: Multi-Function Lever provides 4 to 10 second delay self-timer, depth of field preview, and mirror-lock capability.

Exposure Measurement: Open aperture, center-weighted, through-the-lens light metering for both automatic and manual modes. Integrated Direct Metering (IDM) system measures light at the film plane via Silicon Photo Diode (SPD): high speed measurements for automatic operation are made off fixed pattern on front shutter curtain, slow speed measurements off curtain pattern and film automatic electronic flash/ambient light measurement with TTL "T"-type flash models. Manual exposure range from EV 1 to EV 19 (ASA 100, f/1.4); stepless automatic-exposure range extends to EV -5.5∞ EV 20 (125 sec. at f/1.2 to 1/2000th sec. at f/22 at ASA 100 under normal temperatures and humidity). Meter activated by light pressure on shutter release with automatic shut-off after 25 seconds. ASA film speed range: ASA 6-3200.

Exposure Compensation: Up to ±2 EV automatic-exposure compensation in automatic mode by dial control; dial indexed at 1/4X, 1/2X, 1X, 2X and 4X with click stops at 1/3 EV positions; red flag appears in viewfinder to indicate dial is off "1X" normal exposure position; dial lock provided at "1X" with push-button release.

Viewfinder: Standard FA-1 eye-level pentaxprism finder features silver-coating and shows 98% vertical, 95% horizontal of picture area plus full data viewfinder display; built-in diopter correction by adjustment screw. Finder removable by release lever.

Viewfinder Display: Tri-color display for TTL measured shutter speeds with green LEDs indicating hand-holdable speeds from 1/2000th second to 1/30th second, yellow LEDs as slow speed warning from 1/15th second to 4 seconds, and red LEDs to indicate overexposure or long time and X synch ready light with TTL and dedicated flash units; blue flag indicates automatic at "A" and manually selected shutter speeds; aperture visible in standard FA-1 finder model.

Focusing Screen: SC-21 standard with center split-image spot surrounded by microprism collar on ground-glass field; fully interchangeable with 8 other focusing screens through the lens mount.

Film Transport: Pentax "Magic-Needle" loading system. Single-stroke, rapid wind lever with 120° throw and 25° standoff angle; built-in shutter-cocked indicator. Accepts Winder LX and Motor Drive LX for automatic film advance and automatic rewind capability.

Exposure Counter: Additive two-way exposure counter moves from loading indicator to "36" with color-coded indexes at "0", "20", "24" and "36"; operates in reverse to indicate precise film location for rewind or tracking of multiple exposures.

Film Rewind: Crank type. Film-rewind button doubles as multiple exposure button to disengage film-advance mechanism. Automatic rewind with Winder LX and Motor Drive LX.

Power Source: Two 1.5-volt alkaline or silver-oxide mini-batteries power all electronic systems in both automatic and manual modes; LED flickers in viewfinder to indicate low battery condition; mirror locks when batteries fail.

Mirror: Large back-swing type, instant-return mirror to virtually eliminate image cutoff with most lenses; lock provision.

Back Cover: Standard camera back with spring catch, built-in film memo holder. Back is fully interchangeable with Dial Data LX, Watch Data LX and LX Bulk Film Magazine.

Body Size: 144.5 mm x 90.5 mm x 50 mm (5.7″ x 3.6″ x 1.9″) with standard FA-1 Finder attached.

Weight: 570 grams (20 oz.) with standard FA-1 Finder and batteries.

Other Features: Optional hand grips, special gaskets to minimize entry of dust and moisture, rubber fittings at base for stability on flat surfaces, interchangeable strap fasteners, tripod-spacer ring for use with very compact or large diameter lenses, neck strap with shoulder pad.

---

exposure system will choose an extremely long exposure.

To put the camera in automatic mode turn the shutter-speed dial to "Automatic". The blue marker on the right side of the viewing screen will move to the "A" setting. The camera will now set the shutter speed automatically for proper exposure at the aperture set on the lens. An LED will light up next to the shutter speed chosen by the camera. If the lens aperture is open too wide for proper exposure, a red LED will light up beside the "A" setting to indicate that you must either stop down the lens or switch to manual operation.

To put the camera into manual mode simply turn the shutter-speed dial away from "Automatic" to the desired shutter speed. A blue marker on the right side of the viewing screen will move beside the number denoting shutter speed set on the shutter-speed dial.

Metering System

The Pentax LX uses an almost-instant reacting Silicon Photo Diode (SPD) cell along with a dual set of mirrors, for its unique "Integrated Direct Metering" (IDM) light measuring system. The first mirror is a "beam-splitting" mirror which both reflects the image up into the pentaprism (and out the eyepiece) and allows light to pass through it to strike the shutter curtain. The second mirror reflects the light striking the shutter curtain down to the metering cell on the floor of the camera.

This metering system is really a combination of two metering systems. The first system measures the light reflected off a computer-designed pattern on the first shutter curtain. This metering system alone is used on exposures at fast shutter speeds. At slower shutter speeds (in automatic mode) the metering system also measures the light reflected from the film itself. This reading from the film itself is also used when the camera is used with Pentax "T" electronic flash units, in order to measure both the light produced by the electronic flash and the ambient (available) light in the room.

An additional feature of this system is the fact that a viewfinder blind is not needed for time exposures or remote-control photography, as it is with many other automatic-exposure cameras. With this system the light is measured inside the camera body, not off the viewing screen.

Care must be taken when using the LX in manual mode with a standard polarizing filter, in order to avoid exposure errors. A slight amount of polarization is characteristic of cameras which use beam-splitting mirrors in front of the metering cell. This doesn't become a problem until a standard polarizing filter is used in front of the camera lens, further compounding the polarization of light reaching the metering cell. The solution is to bracket your exposures up to two stops when using a polarizing filter, or change the camera to the automatic-exposure mode. In automatic mode the metering system continues to read the light falling on the film after the instant-return (beam-splitting) mirror has swung out of the way.

Shutter System

The Pentax LX has an electro-mechanical, horizontal-run, metal, focal-plane shutter. This shutter is made of titanium to provide long-lasting durability and resistance to extreme temperature changes.

In automatic mode this shutter provides a range of speeds from just over two minutes to 1/2000 sec. This is a "stepless" range, meaning that speeds between conventional shutter speeds (such as 1/250 sec., 1/500 sec., or 1/60 sec.) will be selected by the camera's metering system to get the exact proper exposure. In manual mode, the camera has a full range of exact, conventional shutter speeds from four full seconds to 1/2000 sec.

Another unique feature of the LX is that all shutter speeds from 1/2000 sec. down to "X" (1/75 sec.) plus "B" are mechanical and can be used when the camera's batteries are exhausted.

There is also a "shutter cocked" indicator next to the shutter-speed dial to remind you to release the shutter tension after using the motor drive or winder.

Electrical System

The electronics of the Pentax LX camera are powered by two 1.5 volt alkaline (LR 44 or equivalent) or silver-oxide (S76 or equivalent) batteries. The camera does not have a separate battery-check feature, but warns you when the batteries are getting low by a flickering LED in the viewfinder. In automatic mode, the mirror will lock when the batteries are completely depleted. To release the mirror, simply move the shutter-speed dial to any of the mechanical shutter-speed settings.

Mirror Lock-up/Self-Timer/Depth-of-Field Preview Lever

The mirror lock-up, self-timer, and depth-of-field preview features are all controlled by the self-timer lever.

Mirror lock-up. The instant-return mirror can be locked up out of the way on the LX. This feature is particularly handy for reducing camera vibration when using very long telephoto lenses or shooting extreme close-ups. *Self-timer.* The self-timer feature of the LX camera is variable from a four to ten second delay, depending how far you turn the self-timer lever. *Depth-of-field preview.* In order to visually preview the depth of field at any given aperture simply push the self-timer lever towards the lens mount.

Flash Synchronization

There are two dedicated, automatic-thyristor, electronic flash units manufactured by Pentax to work in conjunction with the LX camera's IDM light-measurement system: the AF-280T and the AF-400T. This IDM system measures both the ambient (existing) light and the amount of light produced by the flash. It measures the ambient light falling on the shutter curtain of the camera right up to the instant of exposure and automatically controls the light output of these flash units. This system eliminates the need for figuring exposure compensation when using filters or other accessories in front of the lens. Both these units (as well as the Pentax AF 200S and AF 160 flash units) automatically set the camera to the proper shutter speed for synchronization, and activate the flash-ready "X" diode in the viewfinder, when attached to the camera's hot shoe.

AF-280T. This is a medium-size unit with a hot-shoe mount and a pivoting flash head. It is powered by four AA batteries, has an angle of cov-

The LX camera with the Pentax AF 280T electronic flash mounted on the camera's hot shoe. This flash has a pivoting flash head for ease of bounce-flash operation, and works in conjunction with the camera's IDM light metering system.

erage equal to a 28 mm lens, and a guide number of 28 with ASA 100 film.

AF-400T. This is a larger, more powerful unit with a guide number of 40 (with ASA 100 film) and variable power settings. It is a handle-mount unit with a pivoting flash head, and can be powered by six C-cell batteries, a high-voltage power pack, or an AC adapter.

The LX camera body has two separate PC cord terminals, and auto-flash contacts, in addition to the hot-shoe on two of the pentaprism viewfinders. These "auto-flash contacts" are for connecting appropriate Pentax flashes to the LX camera's automatic shutter-speed synchronization feature and IDM metering system, when using the flashes off camera or with a finder which does not have a hot-shoe.

Multiple Exposures

Multiple exposures can be made with the LX by using the film-rewind button on the base of the camera. When you press this button neither the film or frame counter will advance while you cock the shutter. Thus, to make a multiple exposure simply press the film-rewind button before stroking the film-advance lever, and shoot a second (or third, or fourth) exposure on the same frame.

The LX has another feature which comes in handy for making multiple exposures. This is the fact that the frame counter works in both directions. As you rewind the film the counter shows what frame you are at. Thus you can shoot a number of exposures on a number of different frames and use the film-rewind lever to go back and add additional exposures on specific frames.

MOTOR DRIVE AND WINDER LX

You have two choices for motorizing your Pentax LX: the Winder LX and the Motor Drive LX. The major differences between these two units are the number of frames-per-second speed at which they work and their power sources.

The Winder LX can be used either for single-frame or continuous exposures at up to two frames-per-second. It is powered by four AA alkaline batteries.

The Motor Drive LX can also be used for either single-frame or continuous exposures, but this unit can operate as fast as five frames-per-second or as slow as 0.5 frames-per-second. It can be powered three ways: with Battery Grip M (which uses 12 AA alkaline batteries), with Ni-Cad Charger Pack M (which takes six hours to completely recharge), or with Power Pack M (for converting AC current).

Both the Winder LX and Motor Drive LX have a convenient automatic film-rewind feature which rewinds a 36-exposure roll of film in just under ten seconds. They also have an end-of-the-roll warning LED, can be used with remote control operation, and can be used at all shutter speeds except "B".

Other Features and Accessories

The LX has the same "Magic Needle" film take-up spool used on many other Pentax cameras.

This spool permits extremely fast and easy film loading.

There are two data backs (Dial Data LX and Watch Data LX) and a 250-exposure bulk-film back available for the LX.

The LX camera has a new type of camera-strap and accessory lugs which permit the camera to be carried in either horizontal or vertical position. In addition there are two accessory hand grips: a standard-shaped grip, and one made out of wood-like plastic which you custom-carve to the exact shape of your hand.

Specially developed sealings and gaskets have been used on all major finder and body joints to make the LX as moisture- and dust-proof as possible. The film-advance mechanism operates on sealed ball-bearings for smooth, reliable operation, even under the most adverse conditions.

The Pentax LX camera body with Motor Drive LX, 250-exposure bulk-film back, and Pentax AF 400T electronic flash unit attached.

## CHAPTER 5

Pentax Lenses

Asahi has been manufacturing camera lenses since 1923, making it Japan's second-oldest lens manufacturer. The company helped set a world standard for screw-mount lenses with the introduction of their Asahiflex I in 1952, the first SLR camera designed and manufactured in Japan. This camera had a 42 mm screw lens mounting which was soon adopted by many of the other major 35 mm SLR camera manufacturers. These "Pentax-mount" lenses could be interchanged between different makes of cameras for several years, up until automatic features were added. Asahi's designers also developed the first multi-layer, lens-coating process, a major step forward in quality lens manufacturing. Super-multi-coating (SMC) has been used on all glass surfaces of SMC-Pentax lenses since June 1972.

Before computers lens design was a laborious, time-consuming process. Normally, the design of a 4-element lens took two or more specially-trained designers several years. Asahi's wealth of experience, combined with new computer technology and an ongoing design program, has now cut this time down to a minimum.

There were 23 Pentax lenses available in 1974. That number has nearly doubled in the last few years. You now have a choice of 43 lenses for your Pentax system. Only the finest optical glass is used and rigid quality controls are maintained throughout the manufacturing process. All Pentax lenses are subjected to a series of tests before they are allowed to leave the factory, and all lenses are guaranteed against defects in manufacture for a full year.

Several other manufacturers also make lenses for use with Pentax cameras. While some other brands are well made, I would suggest making thorough tests to be sure the lens you are considering buying functions properly.

LENS FACTORS

The popularity of the SLR camera is due partly to its allowing us to see exactly what we are recording up to the moment of exposure. Also important are the ease of operation and the degree of creative control which interchangeable lenses make possible. Lenses are the tools which enable you to "make pictures", instead of just taking them. Let's take a look at some of the factors involved in choosing lenses for your camera:

Focal Length

The focal length of a lens is the distance from the optical center of the lens (when focused at infinity) to the film plane. All lenses are designated by their focal length in millimeters (mm). They are classified in the following major categories: normal (standard), wide-angle, or telephoto. Lenses which are shorter than normal focal length are

These are a few of the Super-Multi-Coated Pentax lenses available for Pentax 35 mm camera bodies. There are 43 to choose from.

considered wide-angles and those having a focal length longer than normal are called telephotos.

Speed

The term "speed" refers to the maximum aperture of the lens. Similar-focal-length lenses often come with different maximum apertures—in different speeds. The faster the lens, the less light you need to use it. Under the same lighting conditions, the faster the lens, the higher shutter speed you can use. Lenses with larger maximum apertures are usually more expensive and bulky than those with smaller maximum apertures, but are often worth the additional expense and weight. Consider the kind of photography you will be doing to determine how fast a lens you need.

Depth of Field

This subject was covered in Chapter 3, but the primary rule to remember is: the shorter the focal length of your lens, the greater the depth of field, the longer the focal length lens, the shallower the depth of field (when all lenses are used at the same aperture).

Image Size

Image size increases or decreases in proportion to the focal length of the lens. The longer the lens, the greater the magnification and the larger the image size; the shorter the lens, the lesser the amount of magnification and the smaller the image size.

Perspective

Perspective is the spatial relation of objects as they appear to the human eye. A common photographic fallacy is the belief that one can change the perspective by changing the focal length of the lens, without changing the camera position. As stated above, the image size is changed by lenses of different focal lengths, but the relative proportions of all the subjects in the picture remain the

These four photographs of downtown Los Angeles, taken from a hillside about six miles away, demonstrate the angle of view of different lenses. The top left was taken with a 50 mm lens (60 degrees). The top right was taken with a 100 mm lens (24.5 degrees). The bottom left was taken with a 200 mm lens (12 degrees). The bottom right was taken with a 400 mm lens (9 degrees).

same and retain the same spacial relationship to each other. *To change perspective, you must move the camera position.* When you move a camera closer to your subject, it changes the size of the subject on film, making it larger in relation to the other objects in the picture. Moving the camera away from the subject (while using the same lens) makes the main subject smaller in comparison to other subject matter.

You can achieve interesting distortions of perspective by getting in close to your subject and shooting from a low angle. The shorter the focal

The picture on the left was taken with a 50 mm lens focused on the round wide-angle mirror insert. Notice how the reflection in the larger mirror and the sand around the mirror are blurred. Stopping the lens down to a smaller opening (photo on right) required the use of a slower shutter speed, but increased the depth of field.

length of the lens, the more extreme the effect. Shooting from a high angle will produce a reversed dramatic feeling. In addition to covering a broader area, a wide-angle lens also creates the optical effect of stretching the apparent distance between the objects in the picture. It makes those from about the middle distance out to infinity appear much smaller as they recede into space. Longer-focal-length lenses have the opposite effect, because they compress the planes in the picture making the subjects appear to be closer to each other. This effect increases as the focal length becomes longer.

THE NORMAL LENS

The focal length accepted by most manufacturers for normal or standard lenses has been 50 mm, which has a 46-degree angle of view. This was based on the fact that the human eye has a 50-degree field of view, and it was felt that this constitutes a comfortable viewing area. However, the technical definition of a normal lens is that the focal length is equal to the diagonal of the film frame. Since the dimensions of the 35 mm film frame are 24 mm × 36 mm, its diagonal measure-

Moving in close with the
35 mm lens elongated the paws
of this gangling puppy,
making a stronger statement.

ment is 43.4 mm. This makes the so called normal 50 mm lens about 15 percent longer than the technical definition says it should be.

In a discussion with some of my colleagues, I found that they prefer the 35 mm as their normal lens, rather than the 50 mm, which they rarely use. This is because the 35 mm's wider coverage and greater depth of field serves them better in many journalistic situations. Asahi's lens designers have come up with a viable alternative to the 50 mm lens. Their compact SMC Pentax-M 40 mm *f/2.8*

lens covers a 56-degree field of view; this is 10 degrees more than the 50 mm lens, and only 6 degrees less than the 35 mm lens.

My suggestion is to try all three lenses, the 35 mm, 40 mm, and the 50 mm. Use them in a situation which represents the type of photography you are interested in doing. Compare the results, and then buy the lens that suits you best. Use it until you have learned its capabilities and its limitations. Do this before you decide on what to purchase next for your Pentax system. Since there is

The SMC Pentax 50 mm f/1.2 lens.   The SMC Pentax-M 40 mm f/2.8 lens.   The SMC Pentax-M 35 mm f/2 lens.

no all-purpose lens which can fulfill all your needs, you will now be better able to decide what lens to buy next: either a wide-angle or a telephoto.

Some additional thoughts to keep in mind when choosing your next lens: When a normal lens is used close to your subject, it has a tendency to distort the nearest objects. This distortion becomes even more pronounced with a wide-angle lens. That is why neither lens is really suited for portraits, though they have many other uses.

Medium-long-focal-length lenses, in the 85 mm to 135 mm range, are the best for portraiture. My personal choice is the 85 mm lens because it brings me close enough to chat with my subject comfortably, while shooting a head and shoulders portrait.

I again urge you to use each new lens until you are completely familiar with its capabilities, before you purchase another. By doing this you will be able to use and enjoy your camera to its fullest capabilities, in the most creative way.

SMC PENTAX LENSES

There are 43 lenses in the current Pentax line. They come with two types of mounts. All lenses are super-multi-coated and fully-automatic.

There are 5 screw-mount SMC Takumar lenses for use with Pentax cameras manufactured prior to the K and M series. In addition, there are 21 bayonet-mount SMC lenses which were brought out with the K-series cameras.

With the introduction of the MX and ME, the

"M" group of miniaturized lenses, which use the K bayonet mount, were placed on the market. On the average, "M" lenses are 20 percent smaller and lighter than previous Pentax lenses, but retain the same high-quality optical standards. The 24 "M" lenses are interchangeable between the K and M-series cameras, however there is no way to adapt any of the bayonet-mount lenses for use on older screw-mount cameras.

ANGLES OF VIEW OF PENTAX LENSES

15 mm	100.5°	50 mm	46°
18 mm	100°	85 mm	29°
20 mm	94°	100 mm	24.5°
24 mm	84°	200 mm	12°
28 mm	75°	400 mm	9°
30 mm	72°	1000 mm	2.5°
35 mm	62°	2000 mm	1°15'
40 mm	56°		

PENTAX TAKUMAR SCREW-MOUNT LENSES

There are still 8 SMC Pentax Takumar screw-mount lenses currently available. They are all super-multi-coated and have fully-automatic operation. They are as follows:

28 mm f/3.5: 7 elements, 75-degree angle of view, minimum aperture f/16, minimum focus 15-3/4 in. (40 cm), weight 7.5 oz. (212 grams), lens hood.

35 mm f/2: 8 elements, 63-degree angle of view, minimum aperture f/16, minimum focus 15 in. (38 cm), weight 8.5 oz. (241 grams), lens hood. Production of this lens was discontinued in 1980, but used models are still available in many photo stores.

35 mm f/3.5: 5 elements, 63-degree angle of view, minimum aperture f/16, minimum focus 18 in. (46 cm), weight 5.3 oz. (150.5 grams), without lens hood.

135 mm f/2.5: 5 elements, 18-degree angle of view, minimum aperture f/22, minimum focus 5 ft. (1.5 m), weight 15.8 oz. (448 grams), with lens hood. Production of this lens has been discontinued, but it is still available in many stores.

135 mm f/3.5: 4 elements, 18-degree angle of view, minimum aperture f/22, minimum focus 5 ft. (65 m), weight 12.4 oz. (351 grams), with lens hood.

200 mm f/4: 5 elements, 12.5-degree angle of view, minimum aperture f/22, minimum focus 8 ft. (2.7 m), weight 19.7 oz. (559 grams), with lens hood.

50 mm Macro f/4: 4 elements, 46-degree angle of view, minimum aperture f/22, minimum focus 9.5 in. (24 cm) (.5x magnification), weight 8.2 oz. (232 grams), lens hood not needed as lens is recessed into mount. This lens is no longer made (as of June 1980), but may be found in the stock of certain camera stores.

100 mm Macro f/4: 5 elements, 24.5-degree angle of view, minimum aperture f/22, minimum focus 18 in. (46 cm) (5x magnification), weight 13 oz. (369 grams), with lens hood.

SMC PENTAX & PENTAX-M BAYONET-MOUNT LENSES

Normal Lenses

SMCP-M 40 mm f/2.8: 5 elements in 4 groups, 56-degree angle of view, minimum aperture f/22, minimum focus 2 ft. (60 cm), weight 3.88 oz. (110 grams). This is Asahi's ultra-compact answer to the more technically correct 50 mm normal lens, as discussed earlier. It is a dramatic example of lens miniaturization, extending just 3/4 in., from the camera body and weighing only 3.88 oz., it is lighter and smaller than any 35 mm lens made. These newer lenses are designated by the "M" after SMCP.

SMCP-M 50 mm f/1.2: 7 elements in 6 groups, 46-degree angle of view, minimum aperture f/22, minimum focus 18 in. (45 cm), weight 13.48 oz. (385 grams). It took years of research by Asahi's engineers to bring you the world's fastest 50 mm lens. It has excellent contrast and resolution for those low-light-level situations, even with slower films, as well as in most normal scenes.

SMCP-M 50 mm f/1.4: 7 elements, 6 groups, 46-degree angle of view, minimum aperture f/22, minimum focus 18 in. (45 cm), weight 8.4 oz. (238 grams). This ultra-compact M-series lens weighs

Rules are made to be broken, so don't trap yourself into a small box of "you should only. . . ." Study what the light is doing to people, places, and things even when you don't have a camera in your hands. There was a nostalgic quality to this scene when I drove by, so I parked the car and walked back to get this high-key, backlighted scene around midday.

20 percent less than most lenses of the same focal length and speed. Although it is a half stop slower than the f/1.2, it is lighter and costs less.

SCMP-M 50 mm f/1.7: 6 elements in 5 groups, 46-degree angle of view, minimum aperture f/22, minimum focus 18 in. (45 cm), weight 6.53 oz. (185 grams). If weight and size are important to you, this very popular M-series lens is 16 percent shorter and 20 percent lighter than the f/1.4. It is a half stop slower, but quite adequate for most low-light-level situations. Moderately priced.

SMCP-M 50 mm f/2: 5 elements in 5 groups, 46-degree angle of view, minimum aperture f/22, minimum focus 18 in. (45 cm), weight 6 oz. (170 grams). It is the normal lens furnished with the Pentax K1000 camera.

Another word of caution in choosing lenses is relevant at this point. A moderate step in focal length is advisable in the choice of your next lens. Jumping to the more extreme focal lengths can be quite confusing. This is true at both ends of the scale, for ultra-wide-angles as well as ultra-tele-photos. Included in the ultra-wide-angle category are 15 mm, 17 mm Fisheye, 20 mm, and 24 mm lenses. Ultra-telephoto lenses are 300 mm, 400 mm, 500 mm, 1000 mm, and 2000 mm.

Wide-Angle Lenses

SMCP 15 mm f/3.5: 13 elements in 12 groups, 111-degree angle of view, minimum aperture f/22, minimum focus 12 in. (33 cm), weight 19.25 oz. (550 grams). This is an ultra-wide-angle lens with maximum coverage and a minimum of distortion. Called a rectilinear lens, it has a special aspherical design which nearly eliminates the curved horizon common with other fisheye lenses. It is particularly useful for architectural photography, for shooting large groups of people, and for wide-spread scenics. You will not have curved horizons or other lines in your pictures like those experienced with the Fisheye lens.

SMCP Fisheye 17 mm f/4: 11 elements in 7 groups, 180-degree angle of view, minimum aperture f/22, minimum focus .66 ft. (20 cm), weight 8.19 oz. (234 grams). This light-weight, full-film frame, fisheye lens allows viewing and focusing through the viewfinder. Unlike many other brands of fisheye lenses it does not require the mirror be raised in order to be mounted on the camera. There are four built-in filters (UV, Skylight, Y2, 02) that are dialed into place, and a built-on gelatin-filter holder at the rear of the lens. This special-purpose lens combines spherical curvature with tremendous depth of field and angle of view, to create wild spatial-distortion effects.

SMCP 18 mm f/3.5: 12 elements in 11 groups, 100-degree angle of view, minimum aperture f/22, minimum focus .79 ft. (25 cm), weight 11.48 oz. (328 grams). This rectilinear lens offers a logical step between the 15 mm f/3.5 and the 20 mm f/4. It has four built-in filters (UV, Skylight, Y2, 02), and it also has a built-on gelatin-filter holder at the rear of the lens.

The SMCP Fisheye 17 mm f/4 lens gives full-frame coverage and has built-in filters.

This dramatic shot of the towers at Century City in Los Angeles was taken with the 17mm Fisheye lens.

SMCP-M 20 mm f/4: 8 elements in 8 groups, 94-degree angle of view, minimum aperture f/22, minimum focus .9 ft. (27 cm), weight 5.29 oz. (150 grams). This compact lens weighs about one-half that of the standard 20 mm f/4 wide-angle lens and is a good choice between a fisheye and a 24 mm lens. The average person may find this lens rather expensive but for the professional photographer who needs the additional 10-degree angle of view when working in a limited access area, it would be a wise investment.

SMCP 24 mm f/2.8: 9 elements in 8 groups, 84-degree angle of view, minimum aperture f/22, minimum focus .79 ft. (25 cm), weight 6.79 oz. (194 grams). A full stop faster than the 20 mm f/4,

it weighs just about the same as the normal 50 mm SMC Pentax f/2 lens.

SMCP 28 mm f/2: 9 elements in 8 groups, 75-degree angle of view, minimum aperture f/22, minimum focus 12 in. (30 cm), weight 14.8 oz. (423 grams). This lens is half-way between the 20 mm ultra-wide-angle and the 35 mm wide-angle lenses. For many photographers the 28 mm is their primary wide-angle choice because it is a good compromise between the normal 50 mm and an extreme wide-angle like the 18 mm lens.

SMCP-M 28 mm f/2.8: 7 elements in 7 groups, 75-degree angle of view, minimum aperture f/22, minimum focus 12 in. (30 cm), weight

5.50 oz. (156 grams). This M-series lens offers compactness with a weight less than half that of the 28 mm *f*/2. It is a stop slower, but costs much less. It is only 1-1/4 in. long.

SMCP-M 28 mm *f*/3.5: 6 elements in 6 groups, 75-degree angle of view, minimum aperture *f*/22, minimum focus 12 in. (30 cm), weight 6.35 oz. (180 grams). The excellent optical performance, compact size, and moderate price have made this the most popular of the wide-angle group. The slower aperture "speed" of this lens is no longer a handicap when you use the new, fast, color films in low light. Flash, or time exposures on a tripod, will be necessary when you use slower films.

SMCP 30 mm *f*/2.8: 7 elements in 7 groups, 72-degree angle of view, minimum aperture *f*/22, minimum focus 12 in. (30 cm), weight 7.52 oz. (215 grams). This lens is a novel step between the 28 mm and 35 mm lenses. It has almost as wide an angle of view as the 28 mm lenses, without having quite as much distortion. The maximum aperture of *f*/2.8 means it is fast enough to be used under almost any lighting conditions.

SMCP-M 35 mm *f*/2: 7 elements in 7 groups, 62-degree angle of view, minimum aperture *f*/22, minimum focus 12 in. (30 cm), weight 7.18 oz. (205 grams). This lens replaced the SMCP 35 mm *f*/2. It has the same lens speed and optical perform-

This photograph of an unusual rock formation near Lake Mead, Nevada, was taken with a 35 mm lens.

This handsome German shepherd was photographed outdoors against a plain wall with an 85 mm lens.

ance as its predecessor, but it is 33 percent shorter and 36 percent lighter.

SMCP-M 35 mm *f/2.8*: 6 elements in 6 groups, 62-degree angle of view, minimum aperture *f*/22, minimum focus 12 in. (30 cm), weight 6.14 oz. (174 grams). This lens is about 20 percent lighter than the *f*/2, and less expensive, but it is a stop slower.

Telephoto Lenses

SMCP-M 85 mm *f/2*: 5 elements in 4 groups, 29-degree angle of view, minimum aperture *f*/22, minimum focus 2.8 ft. (85 cm), weight 8.82 oz. (250 grams). As mentioned earlier, this is a great lens for portraiture, for photographing children and animals, and for pulling in selective details of a landscape.

SMCP-M 100 mm *f/2.8*: 5 elements in 5 groups, 24.5-degree angle of view, minimum aperture *f*/22, minimum focus 3.3 ft. (1m), weight 7.88 oz. (225 grams). Even though this lens is 15 mm longer in focal length than the 85 mm, it is shorter in physical length, (only 2-1/2 in. long) and weighs 32 percent less. It is an ideal moderate telephoto for portraits, amateur theatrical performances, and little league sports. Selective focusing at the widest aperture enables you to eliminate unwanted backgrounds.

SMCP 120 mm *f/2.8*: 5 elements in 4 groups, 21-degree angle of view, minimum aperture *f*/32, minimum focus 4 ft. (1.2 m), weight 9.52 oz. (275 grams). This is another intermediate telephoto lens, midway between the 85 mm and the 150 mm, in both focal length and lens speed.

SMCP 135 mm *f/2.5*: 6 elements in 6 groups, 18-degree angle of view, minimum aperture *f*/32, minimum focus 5 ft. (1.5 m), weight 17.04 oz. (483 grams). This is one of the fastest of the SMCP telephoto lenses. It is well balanced and only 3.38 in. long, making it ideal for shooting available-light sports events, theatre, or other performances where flash is not allowed.

SMCP-M 135 mm *f*/3.5: 5 elements in 5 groups, 18-degree angle of view, minimum aperture *f*/32, minimum focus 5 ft. (1.5 m), weight 9.74 oz. (276 grams). Just about a stop slower than the *f*/2.5, this lens is quite a bit lighter and only 2.58 in. long. It comes equipped with a built-in collapsible lens shade. Consider the advantages of cost and weight versus lens speed when shopping for a 135 mm lens.

SMCP-M 150 mm *f*/3.5: 5 elements in 5 groups, 17-degree angle of view, minimum aperture *f*/32, minimum focus 6 ft. (1.8 m), weight 10.23 oz. (290 grams). This unique lens delivers three times the magnification of the normal 50 mm lens. It is lightweight and easily hand-held, even at 1/125 sec. It is ideal for following sports action, and for close-ups of distant subjects.

SMCP 200 mm *f*/2.5: 6 elements in 6 groups, 12-degree angle of view, minimum aperture *f*/32, minimum focus 6.5 feet (2 m), weight 33.51 oz. (950 grams). This lens is the first 200 mm with an *f*/2.5 maximum aperture. Only 5.70 in. long, it provides 4× the magnification of the normal 50 mm lens.

SMCP-M 200 mm *f*/4: 6 elements in 5 groups, 12-degree angle of view, minimum aperture *f*/32, minimum focus 6.5 ft. (2 m), weight 14.11 oz. (400 grams). If portability is a problem, here is the solution. This lens is only 4.37 long and weighs less than half that of the *f*/2.5. Good for candid photography outdoors, and sports events of all kinds.

SMCP 300 mm *f*/4: 7 elements in 5 groups, 8-degree angle of view, minimum aperture *f*/32, minimum focus 13 ft. (4 m), weight 35.98 oz.

(1020 grams). This telephoto lens provides 6 times the magnification of the 50 mm normal lens. The shallow depth of field, narrow angle of view, combined with the compression effect typical of longer-focal-length lenses, provide a creative tool with which you can dramatically isolate your subject from distracting backgrounds or foregrounds.

SMCP 400 mm *f*/5.6: 5 elements in 5 groups, 6-degree angle of view, minimum aperture *f*/45, minimum focus 27 ft. (8 m), weight 2.7 lb. (1.2 kg). Another compact lens which is light enough for handheld shooting if you use a shutter speed of at least 1/500 sec. A tripod is necessary when using slower shutter speeds. Ideal for sports, wildlife, and news events.

SCMP-M 400 mm *f*/5.6: 5 elements in 5 groups, 6-degree angle of view, minimum aperture *f*/45, minimum focus 17 ft. (5 m), weight 2 lb. 11 oz. (1.22 kg). This improved version of the previous lens has fully-automatic operation and can focus as close as 17 ft. It weighs a little less and is slightly smaller than the manually-operated 400 mm lens.

SMCP 500 mm *f*/4.5: 4 elements in 4 groups, 5-degree angle of view, minimum aperture *f*/45, minimum focus 35 ft. (10 m), weight 7.29 lb. (3.3 kg). Designed for the professional photographer, this lens requires a sturdy tripod to anchor it securely. It has a built-on sight making it easier to align the lens with the subject, since this can be a problem because of the lens's narrow angle of view. There is also a rugged tripod collar built-on the lens, and it comes with a lens shade and case.

SMCP 1000 mm *f*/8: 5 elements in 5 groups, 2.5-degree angle of view, minimum aperture *f*/45, minimum focus 100 ft. (30 m), weight 11.49 lb. (5.25 kg). With 20-times magnification, it is possible to recognize a person being photographed from a distance of 1/8 mile away. This giant utilizes a rack-and-pinion focusing system and has its own specially designed, wooden tripod.

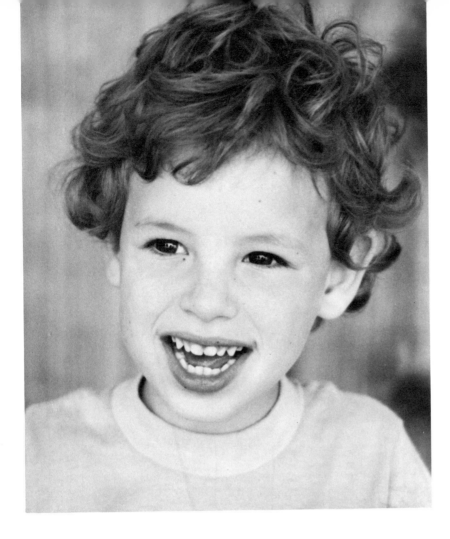

Active youngsters don't like to keep still, so where possible I use fast shutter speeds and a zoom lens. Here the light was late-afternoon sun reflected from the side of a house.

Mirror-Reflex Lenses

Asahi's optical designers used mirror-reflex (catadioptric) design to dramatically decrease the size and weight of the two ultra-telephoto lenses described below. Using front-surfaced mirrors to reflect the light rays that enter the lens, they eliminated many of the problems that require correction in the design of standard, glass-refracting lenses. There is a drawback however, mirror-reflex lenses have just one aperture. Neutral-density filters must be used to control the amount of light reaching the film, instead of an aperture control.

SMCP Reflex 1000 mm *f*/11: 6 elements in 4 groups, 2.5-degree angle of view, minimum aperture *f*/11, minimum focus 27 ft. (8 m), weight 5.03 lb. (2.3 kg). This reflex lens is about 1/3 the length of the 1000 mm *f*/8 and less than 1/2 the weight.

The minimum focusing distance of 27 ft. equals that of most 400 mm lenses but adds 2.5 times magnification.

SMCP Reflex 2000 mm *f*/13.5: 6 elements in 4 groups, 1-degree angle of view, minimum aperture *f*/13.5, minimum focus 65.61 ft. (20 m), weight 17.64 lb. This is the longest lens in the Pentax line and has 40 times the magnification of the normal 50 mm lens. You can pull objects into focus that are barely visible to the naked eye and focus as close as 65.61 ft. Because of the mirror-reflex optical principles, this lens is 8 in. shorter, and its weight is just 6.16 lb. more, than the 1000 mm *f*/8 telephoto. It has built-in, rotating filters and uses 4 rotating neutral-density filters to control exposure. It comes equipped with a built-in lens shade, a rotatable tripod socket, a lens sight, and a light-weight, metal-alloy, trunk-type carrying case.

PENTAX LENSES

Type	Lens	Minimum Aperture	Angle of View (Degrees)	Construction (Groups-Elements)	Diaphragm	Minimum Focusing Distance (m)	Minimum Focusing Distance (ft)	Maximum Diameter & Length (mm × mm)	Weight (gr)	Weight (oz.)	Filter Size (mm)
Fish-eye	SMC Pentax Fish-Eye 17 mmf/4	22	180	7—11	FA	0.2	0.66	64.5 × 34	234	8.19	BI
Ultra-wide-angle	SMC Pentax 15 mm f/3.5	22	111	12—13	FA	0.3	1.0	80 × 81.5	550	19.25	BI
	SMC Pentax 18 mm f/3.5	22	100	11—12	FA	0.25	0.79	63 × 61.5	328	11.48	BI
	*SMC Pentax-M 20 mm f/4	22	94	8—8	FA	0.25	.9	63 × 29.5	150	5.29	49
	SMC Pentax 24 mm f/2.8	22	84	8—9	FA	0.25	0.79	63 × 41.5	194	6.79	52
Wide-angle	SMC Pentax 28 mm f/2	22	75	8—9	FA	0.3	1.0	62.5 × 69	423	14.8	52
	*SMC Pentax-M 28 mm f/2.8	22	75	7—7	FA	0.3	1.0	63 × 31	156	5.50	49
	*SMC Pentax-M 28 mm f/3.5	22	75	6—6	FA	0.3	1.0	63 × 31.5	180	6.35	49
	SMC Pentax 30 mm f/2.8	22	72	7—7	FA	0.3	1.0	63 × 39.5	215	7.52	52
	*SMC Pentax-M 35 mm f/2	22	62	7—7	FA	0.3	1.0	63 × 42	205	7.18	49
	*SMC Pentax-M 35 mm f/2.8	22	62	6—6	FA	0.3	1.0	63 × 35.5	174	6.14	49
Standard	*SMC Pentax-M 40 mm f/2.8	22	56	4—5	FA	0.6	2.0	63 × 18	110	3.88	49
	SMC Pentax 50 mm f/1.2	22	46	6—7	FA	0.45	1.5	65 × 48.5	385	13.48	52
	*SMC Pentax-M 50 mm f/1.4	22	46	6—7	FA	0.45	1.5	63 × 37	238	8.4	49
	*SMC Pentax-M 50 mm f/1.7	22	46	5—6	FA	0.45	1.5	63 × 31	185	6.53	49
	*SMC Pentax-M 50 mm f/2	22	46	5—6	FA	0.45	1.5	63 × 31	170	6.0	49
Telephoto	SMC Pentax-M 85 mm f/2	22	29	4—5	FA	0.85	2.8	62.5 × 46	250	8.82	49
	*SMC Pentax-M 100 mm f/2.8	22	24.5	5—5	FA	1.0	3.3	62.5 × 55.7	225	7.88	49
	SMC Pentax-M 120 mm f/2.8	32	21	4—5	FA	1.2	4	62.5 × 74.5	275	12.43	52
	SMC Pentax 135 mm f/2.5	32	18	6—6	FA	1.5	5	67.5 × 85.9	470	16.45	58
	*SMC Pentax-M 135 mm f/3.5	32	18	5—5	FA	1.5	5	62.5 × 65.7	276	9.74	49
	*SMC Pentax-M 150 mm f/3.5	32	17	5—5	FA	1.8	6	62.5 × 75	290	10.23	49
	SMC Pentax 200 mm f/2.5	32	12	6—6	FA	2.0	6.5	89 × 145	1019	35.9	77
	*SMC Pentax-M 200 mm f/4	32	12	5—6	FA	2.0	6.5	63.5 × 111.0	405	14.18	52
Ultra-telephoto	SMC Pentax 300 mm f/4	32	8	5—7	FA	4	13	85 × 188	942	32.97	77
	SMC Pentax-M 400 mm f/5.6	45	6	5—5	FA	8	16.4	82.5 × 276.5	12 27	43	77
	SMC Pentax 500 mm f/4.5	45	5	4—4	MO	10	35	126.5 × 440	3330	116.6	52
	SMC Pentax 1000 mm f/8	45	2.5	5—5	MO	30	100	143 × 738	5250	183.8	52
	SMC Pentax Reflex 1000 mm f/11	—	2.5	4—6	ND	8	26.24	119 × 248	2300	80.5	BI/52
	SMC Pentax Reflex 2000 mm f/13.5		1.15	4—6	ND	20	65.61	180 × 533.4	8000	282.24	52
Zoom	*SMC Pentax-M Zoom 24 mm/35 mm f/3.5	22	82.5—64.5	9—9	FA	0.5	2	64 × 48	290	10.2	58
	*SMC Pentax-M Zoom 28 mm/50 mm f/3.5 f/4.5	22	75—46	10—10	FA	0.6	2.1	65 × 52	315	11.11	52
	*SMC Pentax-M Zoom 35 mm/70 mm f/2.8 f/3.5	22	62—34	7—7	FA	1	3.25	67 × 76	470	16.45	67
	SMC Pentax Zoom 40 mm/80 mm f/2.8 f/4	22	57.2—30.9	7—7	FA	1.2	4	63.5 × 76	389	13.9	49
	SMC Pentax Zoom 45 mm/125 mm f/4	22	50.5—20	11—14	FA	1.5	5	69 × 127	612	21.42	67
	*SMC Pentax-M Zoom 75 mm/150 mm f/4	22	32.1—16.5	9—12	FA	1.1	3.93	63.5 × 111	456	16.28	49
	*SMC Pentax-M Zoom 80 mm/200 mm f/4.5	32	30—12	12—15	FA	1.6	5.5	65 × 141.5	555	19.57	52
	SMC Pentax Zoom 135 mm/600 mm f/6.7	45	18—4	12—15	MO	6	20	105 × 582	4070	142.5	52
Macro	*SMC Pentax-M Macro 50 mm f/4	32	46	3—4	FA	0.234	0.77	63 × 42.5	160	5.6	49
	*SMC Pentax-M Macro 100 mm f/4	32	24.5	3—5	FA	0.45	1.48	64.6 × 77.5	355	12.43	49
	SMC Pentax Bellows 100 mm f/4	32	24.5	3—5	FA/M	—	—	60 × 40	186	6.51	52
Shift	SMC Pentax Shift 28 mm f/3.5	22	75	11-12	MO	0.3	1.0	80 × 92.5	611	21.39	BI

BI . . . Filters built-in   FA . . . Fully Automatic   MO . . . Manual Operation   ND . . . ND filters built-in

* . . . Compact lens   + . . . Supplied with K 1000

The photograph above was shot with a 40 mm lens. The play of light on this vegetation caught my eye during a stroll along the beach in northern California.

Blurred action is one of the creative techniques you can use to give the feeling of motion.

Zoom Lenses

Zoom lenses provide a variety of focal lengths in one package. They offer the ability to change the field of view and image size of your subject from the same camera position, without changing lenses, providing greater creative control and faster operation. Pentax zoom lenses can hold a point of focus throughout their zoom range, thereby eliminating the need to refocus each time the focal length is changed. Another advantage to zoom lenses is the size and weight. This is usually less than the total of the number of single-focal-length lenses it combines.

Several years ago, zoom lenses had a bad reputation because they were not as sharp as individual-focal-length lenses. This is no longer a problem. Their sharpness now equals any single-focal-length lens. You should bear in mind, though, that zoom lenses weigh more, are bulkier, and have smaller minimum-apertures than individual single-focal-length lenses.

There are eight zoom lenses in the Pentax line:

SMCP Zoom M 24 mm—35 mm f/3.5: 9 elements in 9 groups, 82.5—64.5 degree angle of view, minimum aperture f/22, minimum focus 1.64 ft (4 cm), weight, 10.2 oz. (289 grams). This wide-angle zoom has an ideal range of coverage for architectural, landscape, and many general photographic situations.

SMCP Zoom-M 28 mm—50 mm f/3.5—f/4.5): 10 elements in 10 groups, 75—46 degree angle of view, minimum aperture f/22, minimum focus 2 ft. (60 cm), weight 11.11 oz. (315 grams). This extremely practical combination covers focal lengths from the 28 mm wide-angle to the 50 mm coverage. If you don't mind the relatively-slow maximum aperture this is one of the most compact and lightweight zooms of its type.

SMCP Zoom-M 35 mm—70 mm (f/2.8—f/3.5): 7 elements in 7 groups, 62—34 degree angle of view, minimum aperture f/22, minimum focus 3 ft. 6 in. (1 m), weight 1.03 lb. (470 grams). Here is another compact zoom for its class, weighing only 3 oz. more than the SMCP 50 mm f/1.2 normal lens. It combines "one/action" zooming and focusing for ease of operation, with high performance optics.

SMCP Zoom-M 40 mm—80 mm (f/2.8—f/4): 7 elements in 7 groups, 57.2—30.9-degree angle of view, minimum aperture f/22, minimum focus 4 ft. (1.2 m) "standard" and 14.5 in. (36.9 cm) "Macro", weight 13.9 oz. (394.5 grams). Another critically-sharp zoom from Asahi's lens designers. It has an ideal range for an alternative to the standard lens, and offers the additional flexibility for creative expression of a Macro setting for focusing as close as 14.5 in. (36.8 cm).

SMCP Zoom 45 mm—125 mm f/4: 14 elements in 11 groups, 50.5—20 degree angle of view, minimum aperture f/22, minimum focus 5 ft. (1.5 m), weight 1.34 lb. (612 grams). If outdoor shooting is your speciality, this zoom ranges from normal to midrange telephoto. It is a fine portrait lens, good for capturing children and animals, and also good for bringing distant travel scenes in range. With a zooming range of 3:1, it allows you to increase image size 3 times.

SMCP Zoom-M 75 mm—150 mm f/4: 12 elements in 9 groups, 32.1—16.5 degree angle of view, minimum aperture f/32, minimum focus 3.93 ft. (9.9 cm), weight 16.28 oz. (459 grams). This is another light, compact, M-series Pentax lens with a focal length coverage most useful for portraits and other medium-length telephoto needs.

SMCP Zoom-M 80 mm—200 mm f/4.5: 15 elements in 12 groups, 30—12 degree angle of view, minimum aperture f/32, minimum focus 5.5 ft. (1.6 m), weight 1.2 lb. (555 grams). Another outstanding zoom lens, this one is very compact and lightweight for its class. Easily hand-held, it weighs only 1.2 lb. and is only 5.57 in. long. An ideal range for sports, wildlife, and candid portraits where fast action is necessary.

SMCP Zoom 135 mm—600 mm f/6.7: 15 elements in 12 groups, 18—4 degree angle of view, minimum aperture f/45, minimum focus 20 ft. (6

The SMC Pentax-M Zoom 24 mm—35 f/3.5 lens.

The SMC Pentax Zoom 45 mm—125 mm f/4 lens.

m), weight 8.91 lb. (4.07 kg). A sturdy tripod is necessary with this zoom lens. Has the same "single/action" operation as the other zooms already described. Good for shooting professional-sports events, news events, and wildlife assignments.

Macro Lenses

Macro lenses differ from regular lenses in their ability to produce optimum sharpness at close distances, including corner-to-corner sharpness at their widest apertures. Regular lenses are designed to deliver optimum performance from a few feet to infinity, and resolution drops off when

they are used close. The optical performance of macro lenses at other distances is close enough to regular lens performance that they can be used for general-purpose photography as well. Both the SMCP-M Macro 50 mm and the SMCP-M Macro 100 mm lenses focus down to 1/2 life-size, and will focus to 1:1 (life-size) when used with the K-series auto-extension tubes. When used with these tubes they will retain full-aperture metering and automatic-diaphragm operation.

SMCP-M Macro 50 mm f/4: 4 elements in 3 groups, 46-degree angle of view, minimum aperture f/32, minimum focus 9.24 in. (23 cm), weight 5.9 oz. (167 grams). This versatile macro lens can

The SMC Pentax-M Macro 50 mm f/4 lens.

The SMC Pentax-M Macro 100 mm f/4.

be used with a reverse adapter to create larger-than-life-size images with unlimited possibilities. (The reverse adapter is described later in this book.) It can also be used as an excellent all around normal lens.

SMCP-M Macro 100 mm f/4: 5 elements in 3 groups, 24.5-degree angle of view, minimum aperture f/32, minimum focus 17.76 in. (45 cm), weight 12.43 oz. (355 grams). The convenience of twice the working distance between camera and subject helps prevent perspective distortion when shooting close-ups of 3-dimensional objects. It also provides more freedom in the placement of lights and reflectors.

SMCP Bellows 100 mm f/4: 5 elements in 3 groups, 24.5-degree angle of view, minimum aperture f/32, weight 6.51 oz. (186 grams). This lens

The SMC Pentax Shift 28 mm f/3.5. This lens was used to take the following two photographs.

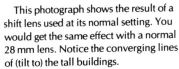

This photograph shows the result of a shift lens used at its normal setting. You would get the same effect with a normal 28 mm lens. Notice the converging lines of (tilt to) the tall buildings.

Here the SMC Shift 28 mm f/3.5 lens was shifted to correct the convergence. Notice how the buildings now appear vertical and parallel. Additional correction can be done, if necessary, by tilting the easel in the darkroom.

requires Pentax-K bellows accessory for macro-photography use because it has no focusing adjustments. This lens has many of the same advantages as the Macro 100 mm f/4 described above.

Shift Lens

SMCP Shift 28 mm f/3.5: 12 elements in 11 groups, 75-degree angle of view, minimum aperture f/32, minimum focus 12 in. (30 cm), weight 1.3 lb. (611 grams). Here is the solution to the perpetual problem of converging lines in architec-tural photography. Convergence occurs when you tilt the camera up in order to be able to include all of the building. When you do this the vertical lines of the building slant inward to the top of the film frame, making the building appear as if it is going to fall over backwards. This lens provides enough movements to correct or intensify the effect. It has a maximum shift of 11 mm, and 360-degree rotation (12 click stops at 30-degree intervals). It also has a built-on lens hood, 3 built-in filters (Y2, 02, Skylight), and a gelatin-filter holder built onto the rear of the lens.

## CHAPTER 6

Auto-Winder and Motor-Drive System

Pentax auto winders and motor drives should have a label reading, "This product can be habit forming, use at your own risk." You will understand why, after using either for just a short time. With an auto winder or motor drive your camera is always ready. The film is advanced and the shutter cocked automatically each time the shutter button is released. This eliminates the distraction of having to take the camera away from your eye after each exposure to wind the film.

Auto winders and motor drives are important tools for the professional and advanced amateur whose specialty is fast action, sports photography, or sequence action for photojournalism. Both pieces of equipment also have many applications in the commercial, industrial, and scientific fields.

Early Pentax motor drives (manufactured prior to the MX) can be used only with specific Pentax camera bodies designed for this purpose. These cameras are marked with an *MD* on the lower-left front of the camera body (the K2DMD is marked on the upper left). *MD* camera bodies are modified models, built to accept the coupling mechanism needed to operate a film-transport system beefed-up for rapid-sequence photography.

The MX camera can be used with either the Motor Drive MX or Winder MX, but the ME camera can only be used with the Winder ME. These camera models do not have the special *MD* marking because both have the strength necessary to handle motorization.

K-Series Motor Drive Units

KX/KM Motor Drive System: This is the basic motor drive unit for modified Pentax KX and KM cameras which use 20- or 36-exposure cartridges. It can also be used with the Bulk-Film-Magazine Camera Back for up to 250 exposures. MD bodies for two earlier Pentax cameras, the ES II and the Spotmatic F, can also be motorized with this unit. Although the KX, KM, ES II and the Spotmatic F cameras are no longer being manufactured, KX/KM Motor Drives are still available. I am including the specifications for those of you who already own one, or are considering the purchase of a used camera and might want to motorize it.

The KX/KM Motor Drive is equipped with a high performance 12-volt DC, micro-motor which can be used with three power sources:

1. Battery Grip with eight standard 1.5-volt penlight batteries. These have enough power for up to 10 rolls of 36-exposure film. This can be increased to 50 rolls, by using alkaline instead of standard batteries. Alkaline batteries cost more, but last much longer.

2. NiCad Battery Pack (type 10/500FZ), is a single 12-volt rechargeable battery which can be used for up to 50 rolls of 36-exposure film when fully charged. It takes 14 hours to recharge a completely discharged battery. These can be recharged about 300 times, and have a maximum life of three years.

Body surfers jumping off a pier were caught in mid-air and mid-water with the help of a motor drive. The action might have been missed otherwise.

3. Other 12-volt, 0.4 ampere, DC power sources, such as automobile batteries, can be used with either a Relay Pack or a Power Pack. The Relay Pack makes multiple camera coverage possible; it also allows time-lapse photography, and remote-control up to a distance of almost four miles. Ordinary AC house current can also be used to power your unit with the Power Pack. The Power Pack can also be used for recharging NiCad batteries.

Additional accessories for the KX/KM Motor Drive unit include: A timer, which is available in three models, (2 to 60 sec., 2 to 60 min., 1 to 24 hrs.), each with the facility for activating a series of lights two seconds before the shutter is released, and automatically turning them off after each ex-

posure has been made (an important feature for time-lapse photography); a 250-exposure bulk film magazine and loader, right-angle finder, two extension power cables (3.84 ft. or 32.80 ft.), and a battery checker.

All shutter speeds including B (bulb), can be used during single-frame operation. Shutter speeds from 1/60 sec. up through 1/1000 sec. are used for continuous-exposure operation at rates from 2 1/2 to 3 frames per second. Mirror lock-up is not required as it is with some other manufacturers' motor drives; the mirror functions normally during both modes of operation.

Motor Drive MD: Designed specifically for the K2DMD camera, Motor Drive MD cannot be

There is less chance of missing a key action shot when you fire the motor drive or winder in short bursts.

used with other Pentax cameras. Like its predecessor, the KX/KM Motor Drive, the MD unit comes in two parts, a motor drive unit and a battery grip.

To attach the unit first remove the coupler cap on the base of the camera using a coin as a screwdriver, then attach the motor drive to the tripod socket by rotating the knurled knob on the front of the unit clockwise. The battery grip provides a firm way of holding the camera, and houses the power source of 12, 1.5-volt, penlight batteries. Standard penlight batteries furnish enough power to expose about 40 rolls of 36-exposure film. This can be increased to about 100 rolls by using alkaline batteries.

Single-frame and continuous-exposure operations can be used throughout the entire range of shutter speeds, from 8 sec. to 1/1000 sec. and bulb. Continuous exposures are steplessly adjustable, from 1/2 to two frames per sec. This unit can be used with the Data Back MD. The Motor Drive MD does not have a battery check, so batteries should be replaced as you approach their limit, or when you hear the unit slowing down. There are speed selectors and shutter-button switches on both the motor drive and the battery grip, thus they can be separated for remote-control operation. Two power cables (3.84 ft. and 32.80 ft.) are available for remote-control operation.

M-SERIES MOTOR DRIVES AND AUTO WINDERS

Motor Drive MX: This model is for use with the Pentax MX camera only. It has the fastest continuous-film-advance speed of all Pentax motor drives, with stepless settings from 1/2 to 5 frames per sec. On the single-frame setting it can be used at all shutter speeds other than bulb, from 1 sec. through 1/1000 sec. In continuous mode the Motor Drive MX can be used with shutter speeds from

1/60 sec. through 1/1000 sec. There are three power sources for this unit:

1. Battery Grip M with 12 alkaline 1.5-volt penlight batteries provides enough power for over 100 rolls of 36-exposure film.

2. NiCad Battery Pack M, when fully charged has enough power for 40 or more 36-exposure rolls. It takes about six hours to recharge when

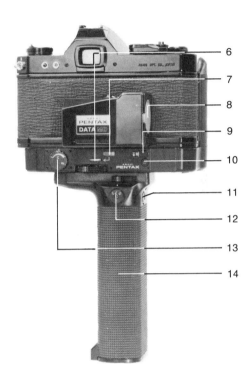

PENTAX MOTOR DRIVE MD (WITH BATTERY GRIP M)
PARTS NOMENCLATURE

1. Trigger release
2. Hand grip
3. Battery Grip M trigger release
4. Motor Drive MD
5. Remote-control socket

6. Exposure-counter dial
7. Exposure counter
8. Data Back MD
9. Film-rewind lever
10. Film-rewind-lever lock button

11. Battery Grip M remote-control socket
12. Battery Grip M C/S dial
13. Motor Drive MD C/S dial
14. Battery Grip M

Remote control of the K2DMD is possible by removing the Battery Grip M and connecting it to the camera and motor drive via an accessory power cable.

The Auto Winder MX can be used in either single-frame or continuous-exposure modes. In the continuous-exposure mode it will fire at up to two frames per second.

fully depleted, can be recharged about 300 times, and has a maximum life of three years. This unit weighs about 20 percent less than Battery Grip M, and is an economical power source if you are doing a great amount of motorized shooting.

3. Power Pack M operates on ordinary AC household current converting it to DC to power the motor drive. It has a built-in timer for unmanned operations such as time-lapse photography, and it can also be used to recharge NiCad Battery Pack M. (A separate Charge Pack M accessory is available solely for recharging the NiCad Battery Pack M.) Although Power Pack M is not necessary for remote-control operation, it must be used if your remote-control power source is AC current.

You can operate the motor drive from a distance of 3.84 ft. (3 meters) or 32.80 ft. (10 meters) with any of the three power sources and either a 3 m or 10 m Power Cable M. Remote-control operation is also possible up to a couple of thousand feet away. To do this you need enough ordinary household (double wire) electrical cord to span the distance from the camera to your control point, and a Remote-Trigger-Connector M. First plug the Remote-Trigger Connector into the motor drive, then connect the household electrical cord to the ter-

minals of the Remote-Trigger Connector. To operate the unit simply short the opposite ends of the extension cord by touching them together.

Winders MX and ME: Auto Winders MX and ME differ from Motor Drive MX in that they are smaller, lighter, and need fewer batteries to operate; but they are limited in the number of frames per second (fps) they can deliver in the continuous mode of operation. Also, neither of the two winders have a provision for remote-control operation. However, they can be modified to accept the 3 m and 10 m Remote-Power Cables, or to be used with a wireless, remote-triggering device. This service is available for a reasonable fee at authorized Pentax service centers.

Auto Winders MX and ME are quite similar in construction and operation, but they are not interchangeable. They can be used with all shutter speeds except bulb. The MX takes four 1.5-volt and the ME needs six 1.5-volt penlight batteries. With both units alkaline batteries will provide enough power for up to 20 rolls of 36-exposure film.

There is a slight difference in the frames per second capability of the two units. The MX operates at up to two frames per second, and the ME at

Motor drives and winders are useful for portraits and short sequences, as well as for sporting events and high-speed situations.

up to 1.5 frames per second. Like the Motor Drive MX, they both have single-frame or continuous operation, controlled by the C/S Dial on the back of the winders. Just to the left of this dial is a red LED (light-emitting diode), which flashes briefly when the shutter is tripped and while the film is being advanced. As a warning, it remains lit if the film should jam. It also lights up after the last exposure on the roll has been made, and the motor makes a clicking sound, to warn that the end has been reached.

Winder ME II

Winder ME II was designed for use with the Pentax MV–1 and ME SUPER cameras, but it can also be used with the ME. It is slightly smaller and weighs .2 oz. less than Winder ME. Although Winder ME II can be used on the ME camera, Winder ME cannot be used on the MV–1 or ME SUPER.

The Winder ME II is quite similar in operation and construction to the Winder ME, but there are some small differences. You can fire the ME II at up to two frames per second (fps), instead of the 1.5 fps of the ME. The Winder ME II also has a remote-control terminal built into the grip. (If you already have a Winder ME and need the remote-control facility, the winder can be modified for this purpose at an authorized factory repair center.)

Winder and Motor Drive Operation

First attach the winder to the camera by removing the film-transport-coupling cover on the bottom of the camera with a coin. (Insert this cover into the small recess provided for it in the winder to keep it from being lost.) Set the C/S dial to *off* and ease the winder into contact with the camera body. Tighten the winder-attachment screw until the camera and winder are securely coupled.

Then, load the camera normally, and advance the first frames manually. Make sure that the film is advancing properly by checking to see if the rewind knob is moving counterclockwise.

For single-frame exposures, turn the C/S dial on the back of the unit to *S.* To fire the camera, press the trigger-release button on top of the grip. You must release the button briefly after firing the camera so the motor can advance the film.

For continuous operation, move the C/S dial to *C,* then press the trigger-release button. The unit

The Winder ME operates at up to 1.5 frames per second and has both single-frame and continuous-exposure capability.

The Winder ME II can be used with the Pentax ME, MV-1, and ME SUPER cameras. It is slightly smaller and lighter than the Winder ME, and operates at up to two frames per second.

These three photographs are part of a sequence taken with the Pentax MX equipped with the Motor Drive MX and a 35 mm lens. The action was photographed at Universal Studios in California. I used a 1/500 sec. shutter speed to stop the action and an *f*-stop chosen by metering for the overall scene. I set the motor drive at five frames per second and photographed three performances to insure my getting adequate coverage.

will keep making exposures and advancing the film as long as the button is depressed, or until the end of the roll.

A word of caution might be advisable at this point. While using both winders, I found that the batteries often conked out when only half of a film frame had been advanced. As a result, I was unable to operate the camera manually, because the shutter-release button and the film-advance lever became immovable. When I replaced the batteries with fresh ones, the film-advance cycle completed itself and the winder and camera worked fine again. The next time this happened I removed the winder from the camera body, which allowed me to use the camera manually. As I have warned previously, if something like this occurs don't ever try to force anything that doesn't move easily on your equipment. You will simply be asking for trouble and a large repair bill.

When you have finished shooting, with either the Motor Drive or the Auto Winders, be sure to turn the C/S dial to *off*. Then release the tension on the shutter mechanism by tripping the shutter-release button, otherwise your shutter will remain cocked until you next use the camera.

Motor drives and winders are rather noisy, so Asahi has made it possible to switch from motorized to manual operation without removing the units from the camera. This is convenient when photographing wedding ceremonies, or other functions, where the much louder, motorized operation would be distracting to the participants. It allows you to get the pictures you want during the ceremony, and return to motorized operation when the situation is appropriate.

## CHAPTER 7

Pentax System Accessories

Your Pentax SLR equipped with a normal-focal-length lens, has the ability to handle a wide variety of photographic situations. There are limits of course, but much of what you can or cannot do depends on your ability to use the camera and lens to their fullest capabilities. It takes a lot of learning and practice, but the knowledge you gain from learning to use your initial equipment will enable you to make a wise choice from the many accessories offered by Asahi. For instance, there are 61 filters in the Pentax Accessory section in the latest dealer's catalog. With experience, you will find that you need a few, but not all. These, along with some of the other accessories, will help you simplify, control, correct, or add to the versatility of your camera's operation. Let's take a look at the Pentax accessories that have not been covered in previous chapters.

Lens Hoods and Caps

These are very important accessories and should be used regularly, because they help protect your lenses from dust, scratches, and fingerprints. The primary purpose of the lens hood is to keep stray light from shining into the lens. This prevents lens-flare patterns and an overall lack of contrast in the photograph. Pentax lens hoods fit on the rim of the lens, and are held in place by a spring mechanism.

Twelve Pentax lenses have built-on lens hoods which slide out for use. Pentax lens hoods come in round and rectangular shapes, both serving the same purpose. *Make sure that you get the proper size lens hood for each lens.* A deeper hood meant for a telephoto lens used on a wide-angle lens will probably result in frames with darkened corners, known as vignetting. This can also happen when you use rectangular shaped lens hoods and are not careful to keep the top and bottom of the lens hood parallel with the top and bottom of the camera.

Front and rear lens caps and a camera-body cap are furnished with each unit. They should *always* be used whenever a lens is removed from the camera body. Keep your lens capped on the camera, when it isn't being used, to protect valuable glass.

Cable Releases

A cable release is a must to prevent camera movement whenever you use the camera on a tripod, copicod, or copy stand. There are three Pentax cable releases. The ten and the twelve inch, with rotating thread mount and locking collar, are useful for long exposures. The double-cable release for the Auto Bellows provides full use of the automatic diaphragm on Pentax lenses, when they are mounted in the normal position.

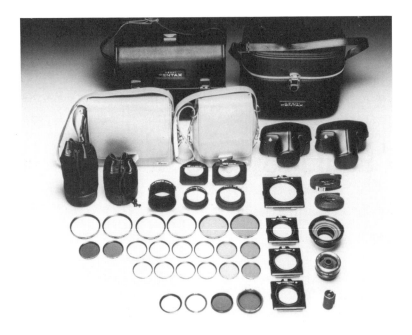

These are only a few of the many accessories Pentax manufactures to help you get the most out of your Pentax camera.

Marine fire fighters practice at their base in Los Angeles harbor. A star filter was used on this photograph to further enhance the reflections of the sun on the water.

PENTAX BLACK-AND-WHITE FILTER CHART

Size	Type	Color	Use
*	UV	Clear	Penetrates haze and fog in distant scenes, at high altitudes and at the beach. Protects lens.
#	Ghostless UV	Clear	Prevents "ghost" images when the light is reflected back through the lens, and as above.
#	Y-1	Light yellow	Gives better rendition of clouds by darkening the sky. Also, gives the most accurate visual rendition of all subjects on B-&-W panchromatic film.
*	Y-2	Yellow	
*	O-2	Medium orange	Darkens blue sky to a greater degree than yellow filters and cuts haze and glare on water surfaces.
#	Y-G	Yellow-green	Corrects color rendering of B-&-W panchromatic film to that of the human eye, ideal for portraits and landscapes.
*	R-2	Medium red	Cuts through haze and mist, darkens the sky dramatically, and can simulate night scenes during the day with a little underexposure.

The basic filter size for the Pentax M and Screw-mount cameras is 49 mm, and for the Pentax K series is 52 mm.

* Available in 49 mm normal coated, and super-multi-coated 49 mm, 52 mm, 58 mm, 67 mm, and 77 mm sizes.
# Available in 49 mm size only.

Colored Filters

Filters are valuable tools for functional and creative control with both B & W and color films. Most filters are made for use with only black-and-white or color film, but a few are effective with both types. A filter works by holding back certain colors of light, including invisible ultraviolet and infrared rays. Thus a filter usually transmits its own color of light, while blocking out complementary colors through absorption. Since the amount of light reaching the film is reduced, additional exposure is necessary, determined by what is called the *filter factor*. However, exposure adjustment is made automatically by through-the-lens metering systems.

As shown on the accompanying filter chart, filters can be used to correct a color-and-film situation, or to provide an effect not otherwise possible. For instance, you can shoot indoor film outdoors with a Type A filter (which converts the film for daylight use). For a special effect, you can add an overall hue to a picture by placing a colored filter (normally used for B&W photographs) in front of the lens. A light yellow (Y-1) perks up an overcast day on color film by giving the feeling of mild sunshine. Try this for scenics or silhouettes when the sky is pale grey or white.

Today's black-and-white films do a fine job reproducing the nuances of grey, but some colors simply do not appear on film as the eye sees them. Using the proper filter can correct this, or add emphasis. The Polarizer is a prime example. It is valuable with both black-and-white and color film because it deepens the blue in the sky, and cuts some reflections, without changing other colors.

Some natural effects benefit from the use of filters, but others should not be disturbed. The color of sunlight, for instance, varies from dawn to dusk, starting and ending red but becoming more blue at midday. Contrary to what you may read in the data packed with color films, don't tamper with the very-warm light of sunset, because its beauty is usually outstanding. In fact, on days when the sun sets in an ordinary manner, try a medium orange (0-2) filter to simulate warmth. You should try combinations of various filters for creative personal expression.

Five SMC Pentax lenses have built-in filters which are dialed into place by turning a ring at the front of the lens. There is a choice of UV, Skylight, Y2, and 02 filters. Gelatin filters, cut to the proper size, can also be used with a filter clip built onto the rear of these lenses. The Pentax lenses that

In the photograph on the left, the store windows reflect the buildings across the street. A polarizing filter was used in the photograph on the right, which eliminated most of the distracting reflection. Polarizing filters can also be used to darken skies and emphasize clouds with both black-and-white and color film.

PENTAX COLOR FILTER CHART

Size	Type	Color	Use
*	Skylight	Light pink	Reduces blue cast outdoors, especially in open shade, and warms all colors slightly.
#	Ghostless Skylight	Light pink	Eliminates ghost images which occur when light is reflected back through the lens, along with the above.
*	Cloudy	Brown	Adds more warmth than Skylight filters, good on an overcast day.
#	Morning & Evening	Light blue	Corrects the excess red of early morning and late afternoon sunlight.
#	Flash	Blue	Corrects color balance of *clear* flash bulbs used with daylight color film.
#	Flood	Blue	Corrects color rendition of daylight film used with photoflood lights.
#	Type A	Amber	Converts Type A indoor film to outdoor use.
+	Fluorescent light	Pink	Corrects the blue-green cast to daylight or indoor film used to take photographs in rooms with fluorescent-lighting fixtures.
+	Fantasic Color R/B	Multi-Color	Provides a continuous variation of colors from red to violet to blue.
+	Fantasic Color R/G	Multi-Color	Provides a continuous variation of colors from red to amber to green.

The basic filter sizes for the Pentax M and Screw-mount cameras is 49 mm, and 52 mm for the Pentax K series.

* Available in 49 mm normal coated, and super-multi-coated 49 mm, 52 mm, 58 mm, 67 mm and 77 mm sizes.
# Available in 49 mm size only.
+ Available in both 49 mm and 52 mm sizes.

This photograph was taken with an 02 orange filter to dramatize the light-colored lines of an addition to the Desert Inn Hotel in Las Vegas. Notice how the orange filter makes the sky turn almost black.

have this convenience are the Fish Eye 17 mm $f/4$, 15 mm $f/35$, 18 mm $f/3.5$, Reflex 1000 mm $f/11$, and the Shift 28 mm $f/3.5$.

Pentax filters are manufactured from the finest optical glass with the same high optical standards as Pentax lenses. The previous Pentax-filter chart lists currently available filters and their uses.

Magic-Image Attachments

Another new addition to the Pentax line, Magic-Image Attachments are a series of five separate, optical-glass filters, each with a varying number of prisms that produce multiple images. You can create a wide range of unusual photographs with these filters by varying focusing techniques and changing the position of your subject in the film frame. A ring on the filter is turned until you see the composition you want in the viewfinder. These can be combined with other filters to create a multiplicity of visually creative statements.

Neutral-Density Filters

A number of manufacturers make filters to fit Pentax lenses. Most of these will perform adequately, though Pentax accessories are made to exacting quality standards to give you a balanced system.

One set of useful filters not being manufactured by Asahi at this time are neutral-density filters. These come with varying degrees of light transmission, usually about one third of a stop apart. They are used to reduce the overall amount of light reaching the film, without changing the tonal values. Neutral-density filters are especially valuable when your camera is loaded with a high-speed film and you wish to photograph a brightly lit subject or scene. A fast film can be slowed by $2\times$, $4\times$ or more, to give you better exposure control. Suppose, when shooting outdoors you want to use the widest aperture of a lens to make the background go out of focus, neutral-density filters will do this job well with either black-and-white or color film.

Focusing may be difficult with any filter mounted on the lens, especially deeper colored ones. However you should focus through the filter for accuracy, since some filters can cause a shift in focus.

Stereo Adapter 49 mm and 52 mm

These accessories will add the feeling of extra visual dimensions to your color transparencies, turning them into three-dimensional pictures when viewed with the Stereo Viewer II. The Stereo

Adapter comes in two sizes, 49 mm and 52 mm, for use with a standard 50 mm or 55 mm Pentax lens. It screws onto the front of the lens, and is held in place with a set-screw. It creates a stereoscopic pair of images on each film frame, and when the film is placed in the Stereo Viewer II you see the dramatic results. Your stereo slides will be most effective when they have an object in the foreground, to give more depth to the scene. If you have never seen three-dimensional slides and want to study their possibilities, slides on various subjects are sold with a special viewer, in gift shops at many amusement centers, camera stores, department stores, etc. by the View Master company.

6 × 7 Lens Adapter

This adapter enables owners of the larger-format 6 × 7 Pentax SLR to use their Pentax 6 × 7 SMCT lenses on Pentax 35 mm SLR's. They can be used on either Pentax bayonet or screw-mount cameras with stop-down metering and manual diaphragm operation. Full exposure automation is retained with any Pentax automatic camera.

Close-up Lenses

There are six SMC-Pentax Close-up Lenses in the Pentax line. These are designed for use with specific SMC-Pentax lenses, as shown in the accompanying chart. They come in three sizes (to fit 49 mm, 52 mm and 58 mm diameter lenses), and are mounted by screwing into the threaded rim that encircles the front of the camera lens.

Pentax Close-up Lenses are marked with the prefix *S* or *T,* followed by a number. *S* indicates close-up lenses which should be used with lenses from the SMC-Pentax 40 mm through the 55 mm. Those marked *T* should be used with longer-focal-length lenses from 85 mm through 150 mm. The number following these letters indicates the focal length of the close-up lens stated in centimeters.

The Pentax 5C Magic Image filter produces multiple images of the subject. The 4C and 2C Magic Image filters do the same thing, but with less multiple images. The object in this photograph is a rusted steel casting photographed against a dark background.

PENTAX BLACK-AND-WHITE AND
COLOR FILTER CHART

Size	Type	Color	Use
#	Polarizer	Gray	Excludes glare and reflections in both color and B-&-W film from windows, water surfaces, and other non-metalic shiny surfaces, and makes the blue in the sky deeper in color film.
+	Magic Image 5C, 4C, and 2C	Clear	Provides multi-images of the same subject. They produce six, five, and three images respectively, and have a rotating ring to change the subject's position in the film frame.
+	Magic Image 6M	Clear	Provides half of the image area for the subject and then repeats that image in five parallel segments in the other half of the frame, for a total of six images.
+	Magic Image CF	Clear	Provides a sharp image in the center of the frame, and a soft, hazy effect around the edges.

The basic Filter sizes for the Pentax M and Screw-mount cameras is 49 mm, and 52 mm for the Pentax K series.

\# Available in 49 mm normal coated, and super-multi-coated 49 mm, 52 mm, 58 mm, 67 mm and 77 mm sizes.
\+ Available in 49 mm size only.
  Available in both 49 mm and 52 mm sizes.

You will get the maximum definition possible by following the recommendations of Asahi's engineers. However, close-up lenses can also be used in combinations to produce larger magnifications. There are limitations to this, since the greater the magnification, the more distortion and loss of sharpness. This is all relative, involving a number of factors, such as the size of the print to be made, how it is going to be used, at what distance it will be viewed, etc. But the most important factor is if the combination answers your needs. It is totally up to you to decide what works best for you with your equipment.

Other manufacturers also make close-up lenses which will fit your Pentax lenses. These are measured in diopters and usually come in sets of

Since my camera was loaded with fast film when I saw this interesting cloud formation I used a neutral-density filter to bring the exposure within the range of the camera controls.

PENTAX SMC CLOSE-UP LENSES
MAGNIFICATION CHART

Close-Up Lens	Thread Diameter	SMCP Lens Recommended	Lens to Subject Distance Range	Magnifi-cation Range
S25	49 mm 52 mm	50 mm f/1.7 50 mm f/1.4 50 mm f/2. 55 mm f/1.8 40 mm f/2.8	8.58″-12.71″ (with 50 mm f/1.7)	.20-.37
S40	49 mm 52 mm	50 mm f/1.7 50 mm f/1.4 50 mm f/2. 55 mm f/1.8 40 mm f/2.8	10.53″-18.72″ (with 50 mm f/1.7)	.13-.28
T80	49 mm 52 mm	85 mm-150 mm	19.70″-35.72″ (with 85 mm f/1.8)	.11-.23
T95	58 mm	135 mm f/2.5 200 mm f/4	32.76″-44.46″ (with 200 mm f/4)	.21-.38
T160	49 mm 52 mm	100 mm-150 mm	34.90″-68.25″ (with 135 mm f/3.5)	.08-.20
T183	58 mm	135 mm f/2.5 200 mmf/4	44.07″-78.78″ (with 200 mm f/4)	.11-.26

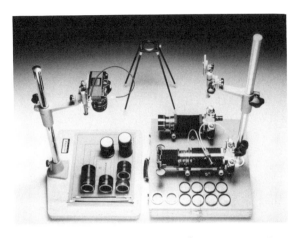
These are just some of the close-up and copying accessories available for your Pentax camera.

This piece of driftwood was photographed at a 1:2 ratio with the Pentax 100 mm Macro lens.

three. They can be used individually or in combination. Additional magnification is possible by using extension tubes in conjunction with close-up lenses.

Extension Tubes (Rings)

Extension tubes provide another reasonably-priced method of getting sharper close-ups, at much higher magnifications than possible with close-up lenses. In addition, you can use your own camera lenses, since there is no need for other optical elements. One of the basic principles of close-up photography states, "The degree of magnification increases as the lens is moved away from the camera's film plane and gets closer to the subject." Extension tubes, or bellows are based on this principle. They are attached to the camera body at one end and to the lens at the other.

Asahi offers several extension tubes and sets of tubes which can be used singly, or in combination with each other or with bellows extensions. These extension tubes are:

Auto Extension Tube Set: Three different size tubes (12 mm, 19 mm, 26 mm) make up this set. They can be used in combination (total 57 mm) or can be used individually. When these are used with Pentax automatic cameras the convenience of automatic-diaphragm operation and open-aperture metering is retained. You can get life-size magnification with the SMC Pentax-M Macro 50 mm lens by attaching the #3 tube, or by using all three tubes with the SMC Pentax-M Macro 100 mm lens. Screw-mount Pentax Takumar lenses can be used with these tubes by adding the Pentax mount adapter. Magnifications range from 1:1 to 1.89:1, with the 50 mm lens.

Manual Extension Tube Set: This set also has three different size tubes (9.5 mm, 19 mm, 28.5 mm). Though they differ in their separate sizes, in combination they add up to the same total of 57 mm. Screw-mount Takumar lenses can be used in conjunction with Mount Adapter B. All lenses require stop-down metering and manual-diaphragm operation with this set. Magnifications range from .95:1 to 1.89:1, with the 50 mm lens.

Helicoid-Extension Tube: This "adjustable extension tube" is a zoom type, with a stepless focusing range from 26.5 mm to 46.5 mm. This gives a magnification range from just over 1/2 life-size (.52) through just over life-size (1.06) with the SMC Pentax-M 50 mm lens. The Helicoid Extension Tube can be used with both the Auto and

The Auto Extension Tube Set (above) consist of three rings which can be used individually, or in combination.

The Helicoid Extension Tube (right) provides variable tube extension with stepless focusing.

Manual-Extension tubes, and can be used for even larger degrees of magnification by combining both units. It will take Pentax screw-mount and lenses with the proper adapters. Manual-diaphragm and stop-down-metering are required with all lenses, but full exposure automation is retained when this tube is used with automatic Pentax cameras.

Life-Size Auto Extension Tubes

Two auto-extension tubes were recently added to the Pentax close-up-accessories line. Designed primarily for use with the SCMP-M Macro 50 mm and the SCMP-M Macro 100 mm lenses, they both offer automatic-diaphragm operation and open-aperture metering with full exposure automation with automatic Pentax cameras. Life-size or larger magnifications are possible when they are used with either of the Macro lenses.

Life-Size Auto Extension Tube (B) 50 mm: When used with the SCMP-M Macro 50 mm lens this tube enables magnifications from life-size to 1:1.5×. (It provides up to life-size when used with the SCMP-M Macro 100 mm lens.) This is an economical alternative to purchasing the entire Auto Extension Tube set. When used with longer-focal-length lenses it allows you to reduce the minimum focusing distances and get larger images at closer range. (About .4× with lenses from 120 mm to 135 mm and about .25× with the 200 mm lens.)

Life-Size Auto Extension Tube (B) 100 mm: With the SCMP-M Macro 100 mm lens this tube produces magnifications from life-size to 1.5×. (It has a magnification range from 1:2× to 1:2.5× with the SCMP-M Macro 50 mm lens.) With the non-Macro 100 mm lens the magnifications will be about 1×, with the 120 mm through 135 mm lenses from .8×, the 200 mm .5×, and the 300 mm lens .35×.

Reverse Adapters

When you are working at magnifications larger than life-size, Asahi recommends reversing the lens to get the best image quality and reduce

Creative control is possible through the use of filters. In this case the bright red blossoms didn't really stand out against the dark background (left) until I used a deep-red (R-2) filter to make the blossoms appear lighter and the background darker (right).

the amount of lens extension needed. (This is due to an optical principal related to the subject's distance from the lens.) Lenses are normally reversed with a reverse adapter which screws into the filter-mounting threads on the front of the lens and is then inserted backwards into the camera body. There are three Pentax adapters available: two bayonet-mount for 49 mm and 52 mm diameter filter threads, and one 49 mm for Pentax screw-thread mount lenses.

Bellows Units

One of the most versatile tools for macrophotography is the bellows-extension unit, particularly when you plan to do a large amount of close-ups. The accordion-like bellows has a mounting ring at one end which you connect to the camera body, and lens boards which accept lenses at the other end. Both ends of the bellows are mounted on a sturdy, single rack-and-pinion track offering variable magnification and continuous fine focusing. Extension tubes can be added between the bellows unit and the lens if you need additional magnification. There are three Pentax Auto Bellows Units available; *Auto Bellows (B), Auto Bellows (B)-M, and Auto Bellows (S)*. Another model with fewer features than the *Auto* units and lower in cost is *Bellows Unit (B)*. The Auto Bellows Units can be paired with *Slide Copier (B)* for duplicating or making creative changes in transparencies.

Auto Bellows Units (B), (B)-M, (S): These units incorporate a lens-reversing feature in their lens boards, and come equipped with a double cable release, operated by a single control, which retains automatic diaphragm operation. (This is not true when the lens is reversed, however, and stop-down metering must be used.) The Auto Bellows extend from 38 mm to 170 mm, providing a magnification ratio from .76× through 3.4×, with the 50 mm lens not reversed. There is a scale which indicates just how far the bellows has been extended. There is an adjustable tripod-mount which rides along the bottom of the rail and is convenient for maintaining balance between the camera body and the lens being used. Screw-mount lenses can be used with a mount adapter on models *(B)* and *(B)-M*.

Auto Bellows (B) will accept all Pentax bayonet-mount lenses in reverse position, but regular step-down adapters cannot be used with this unit.

Auto Bellows (B)-M comes equipped with a removable 49 mm diameter lens adapter so that most SCMP-M 49 mm filter size, bayonet-mount lenses can be used. When you remove this adapter, 52 mm diameter lenses can be used in reverse position.

Auto Bellows (S) is for use with all Pentax screw-mount and universal thread lenses, and will accept 49 mm screw-mount lenses in reverse position. Regular step-down or step-up adapters cannot be used with this unit.

Bellows Unit (B): This unit is a budget model similar to Auto Bellows (B), but with fewer features. It does not have the following: double cable release, as much bellows extension (31 mm to 135 mm as compared to 38 mm to 170 mm), it does not permit automatic diaphragm setting, and it cannot be used with Slide Copier (B). A reverse adapter must be used when lenses are used in reverse position. Bellows Unit (B) has a magnification ratio from .62× to 2.7×, and Pentax screw-mount and universal thread lenses can be used with Mount Adapter (B).

Slide Copier (B) for Auto Bellows Units: If you wish to make duplicate slides, blow up a portion of a transparency, correct or add color, Asahi's Slide Copier (B) is a convenient unit which you fasten to the front of any one of the Pentax Auto Bellows Units. Using the standard 50 mm lens you get the 1:1 magnification necessary to make duplicate transparencies, and up to 1:1.5 by reversing the lens. This magnification is necessary when you wish to crop or blow up a part of a transparency. The slide can be moved in the carrier from side to side, and the unit has its own bellows for moving the slide closer or away from the lens. You can also make color or black-and-white negatives from your color transparencies, either mounted or unmounted.

The slide carrier is behind a sheet of frosted glass for even illumination. A variety of light sources can be used, depending on the type of copying film and the effect you wish to achieve.

The Bellows Unit B attached to a Pentax ME.

Slide Holder 1× (B): If you don't own a bellows, Asahi has another accessory for copying transparencies. This is the Slide Holder 1× (B) which attaches to Pentax 50 mm lenses. You do need a set of auto extension tubes, or a reverse adapter with the standard 50 mm or Macro 50 mm lens to get 1:1 magnifications. The procedure is to attach the extension tube to the camera body, then the reverse adapter is attached to the extension tube. This receives the reversed lens, and the Slide Holder is placed on the rear lens mount.

Macro Focus Rail III: One of the major problems experienced in close-up photography is shallow depth-of-field. One solution is careful focusing and using the smallest aperture possible. Asahi's Macro Focus Rail III provides convenient, precision focusing where it is most needed. It moves the whole camera to the proper position. This is very useful in set-ups with a predetermined magnification, since moving just the lens causes a change in degree of magnification. This unit has a double rail for rigid support.

I used a Y-2 filter to bring out the clouds in this scenic view of Lake Tahoe, California.

Critical Focusing Aids

Rubber Eyecups: These fit on the camera's eyepiece and are a big help in eliminating reflections in the viewfinder. They also help prevent extraneous light from entering the eyepiece, which could influence the exposure metering system.

Magnifiers—Magnifier and Magnifier-M: These are clip-on magnifiers which fasten to the grooves of the camera eyepiece. They magnify the central portion of the focusing screen 2× and are a must for critical focusing. They are hinged to raise out of the way. Diopter correction lenses in your eyeglass prescription can also be used.

Right-Angle Finders (M)—(II): The Right-Angle Finder, also known as a Refconverter, is an invaluable aid when you are using the camera on a tripod, or copy stand, and are shooting down on your subject. Indeed, these two models are useful in any situation where it is difficult to see your subject with normal eye-level viewing. One such situation is shooting over people's heads at a parade. With the Finder, you can raise your camera upside down with your arms extended over your head to get a clear view and pictures. Both models provide the same image you normally see in the viewfinder. They come equipped with eyecups and have a provision for diopter adjustment. Right-Angle M has a built in 2× magnifier activated by a switch.

Right-Angle Finder 1: This is a less expensive version of the Right-Angle Finders M and II. It is made to be used with the K series cameras only. It has one drawback in that the viewing image is seen in a reversed position. Since the figures on the shutter-speed scale and/or aperture read-out in the viewfinders of the KX, K2 and K2DMD will appear backwards in this finder, it is only recommended for use with the Pentax K1000 or KM. It will not fit the MX or ME.

Film Magazine (cartridge)

If you use your camera often, loading your own film magazines from bulk-film rolls can help cut your photographic expenses substantially. Many camera stores carry 100-foot rolls of film in stock, or they will order them for you. You will need an inexpensive bulk-film loader to load film magazines. The process is simple and once the bulk film has been placed in the loader, (in a darkroom, lightproof closet, or a changing bag) the film magazines can be loaded in normal room light. A 100-foot roll of film will give you about 18 rolls of 36 exposure film. Pentax film magazines are made of metal and should last a lifetime.

Camera and Lens Cases

Most Pentax lenses come in their own hard-leather cases. If you should lose a case, replacements are available for most Pentax lenses. In addition, there are two sizes of soft, buckskin-leather cases which take up less space than hard-leather cases.

Asahi has come up with a unique concept in camera case design which allows you to custom fit your ME or MX camera case to the specific lens being used on the camera. The case comes in two parts, a standard back into which you slide the camera, and several ever-ready front cases molded to fit the size and shape of various lenses. There is another case for the MX and ME fitted with the Auto Winder and one for the Dial Data Back. The Quiet/Action Case is an interesting way of reducing camera-operation noise when shooting stage performances, wildlife, or anywhere you don't wish to draw attention. This case covers everything but the camera lens and controls.

ME Belt Clip

Another convenient method for carrying your Pentax ME is the Belt Clip. This can be used instead of a neckstrap. It is a sturdy metal clip that fastens to the camera's tripod socket and clips onto your belt.

Camera Straps

All new Pentax cameras are furnished with an adjustable neckstrap and shoulder pad. Replacement straps and "D" Rings, for fastening them to the camera body, are available.

Hand straps can be used instead of neckstraps, and are fastened with "D" Rings to the camera body.

Slide Holder 1X.

Which filter did I use on this marina scene? The answer is none. Thick, dark, heavy-looking clouds don't usually need filtration. In fact, if you keep your negative density reasonably thin by slightly underexposing, the overall print quality improves, and you rarely need filtration to make the clouds show.

Tripod 1000

I have explained earlier the importance of using a tripod for close-up photography, with long-focal-length lenses, and any time you want to be sure of getting vibration-free photographs. Asahi designed the Tripod 1000 specifically for use with the SCMP 1000 mm f/8 lens. This rugged tripod of wood and metal construction comes with its own carrying case. It is fully adjustable in height from 36 inches to 53 inches, and is 45 inches long when folded for carrying.

Gadget Bags

For maximum protection and convenience Pentax has two gadget bags made of water-resis-tant, long-wearing plastic. The Deluxe Gadget Bag was specially designed for the compact cameras. It has two compartments, one above the other. The lower compartment opens separately and holds a camera, lens, and winder or motordrive. The top compartment has room for two "M" series lenses up to 200 mm long, an AF-16 Electronic Flash Unit, and a variety of film, filters, and accessories.

The SLR 500 Gadget Bag is a larger, felt lined, case with a removable shelf that has molded supports to hold a camera and a standard lens. This bag also has adjustable partitions to hold a variety of lenses and other accessories. A special cut-out allows you to place a long telephoto lens under the shelf compartment. Filters can be stored in their own special holder in the top of the cover.

## CHAPTER 8

Flash Photography

WHEN IS FLASH NEEDED?

1. At family gatherings, parties or other affairs, when you want to be able to move around to get informal, candid, shots and can't depend on the quality of the existing light.

2. In low-light-level situations where you wish to capture fast action.

3. In low-light-level situations where if you use a lens at its widest apertures, the depth of field would be too shallow.

4. If the quality of the existing light is unacceptable photographically, as it is with high ceiling lights. These give your subjects "black eye" because of the shadows they cast.

5. When you are shooting in a room with large windows, and want to match the outdoor light to achieve a proper balance in the final print or slide.

6. For back-lighted subjects outdoors, to illuminate the dark shadows and lower picture contrast.

FLASH BULBS OR ELECTRONIC FLASH?

The accompanying flash-synchronization chart will help you decide which type of flash best answers your needs with a Pentax SLR camera. Factors that should be considered are as follows:

Flash Bulb Units

Most still available flash-bulb units are small and compact. They cost less than their electronic flash counterparts, but you have to keep feeding them flash bulbs for each exposure. A large supply of bulbs must be carried with you, particularly on long trips, and will take up space in your gadget bag which could be used for other equipment. There is the disposal problem too, after the bulbs have been used.

There are some advantages to flash-bulbunits,

though. Certain flash bulbs have higher guide numbers (GN) than pocket-size and medium-size electronic flash units, and are useful for lighting up large areas, or when you want more depth of field. Some professionals carry a small flash-bulb unit when traveling, as a back up in case something should happen to their electronic unit.

Electronic Flash Units

There has been such a proliferation of portable, compact, electronic-flash units that the May 1980 issue of Modern Photography magazine had an article listing and comparing 126 automatic flash units. There are probably more models available now, including Asahi's Pentax AF 280T and AF 400T which weren't listed.

This candid moment at a social affair was captured by a Pentax AF-16 electronic flash unit mounted on a Pentax camera.

FLASH SYNCHRONIZATION CHART

Camera	Camera Body Sync. Terminals		Cordless Hot-Shoe Mount	X Sync. Shutter Speeds	Flash Bulb Sync. Shutter Speeds	
	PC	X			FP	X
MV	No	No	Yes	1/100 sec.	Bulb Only	Bulb Only
MV-1	No	No	Yes	1/100 sec.	Bulb Only	Bulb Only
ME Super	No	Yes	Yes	1/125 sec.	Bulb Only	Bulb Only
ME	No	Yes	Yes	1/100 sec.	Bulb Only	Bulb Only
MX	Yes	Yes	Yes	1/60 sec.	1/60- 1/1000	Bulb- 1/15
K1000	No	Yes	Yes	1/60 sec.	Bulb Only	Bulb- 1/30
K2	Yes	Yes	Yes	1/125 sec.	Bulb- 1/1000	Bulb- 1/15
K2 DMD	Yes	Yes	Yes	1/125 sec.	Bulb- 1/1000	Bulb- 1/15

Bounced flash eliminated the harsh shadows which would have resulted from direct flash with the subjects so close to the walls.

PENTAX AF-16 ELECTRONIC FLASH

Asahi's Pentax AF-16 is literally a pocket-sized unit, designed to match the scale of today's smaller, lighter, compact SLR cameras. It is only 2.6 inches wide, 3.1 inches high, 1.6 inches deep, and weighs 5 oz. including batteries. This unit mounts onto your camera's hot shoe. It allows either manual or automatic operation. A built-in electronic sensor controls the flash output for consistently fine exposures within its auto-flash range. You have a choice of two f-stops which vary according to the ASA rating of the film being used: they cover a distance range of either, 1.5 ft. to 13.12 ft. or 3.28 ft. to 19.68 ft.

The AF-16's flash duration ranges from 1/1000 to 1/40,000 of a sec., depending on how close you are to your subject. An important feature is its wide angle of illumination which covers the area seen by a 28 mm lens. Two AA alkaline penlight batteries provide enough power for up to 200 flashes. Ordinary carbon batteries can be used, but are only good for up to 40 flashes. Ni-Cad batteries cannot be used in the AF-16 because of different voltage ratings and characteristics. The AF-16 has a GN of 24 with ASA 25 film.

Operating the AF-16 in either mode is simple. For automatic operation you turn the Auto/Manual output selector, on the side of the unit, to either the red or blue dot, depending on the distance you wish to cover. Then, using the exposure table on the back of the unit, set the lens aperture to the f-stop listed above the ASA of the film you are using. Turn the power switch on. The combined Open-Flash/Pilot Lamp (ready-light) should light up in about six seconds and you are ready to take pictures. As the power in the batteries is used up, the recycling time will get progressively longer. Batteries should be replaced when it takes over 60 seconds for the pilot lamp to come on, or when you no longer hear the high pitched sound of the batteries charging.

PENTAX AF 200S ELECTRONIC FLASH

The Pentax AF 200S is a dedicated, automatic-thyristor, electronic-flash unit which was designed specifically, for simplified automatic operation with the Pentax MV camera; it also synchronizes automatically with the MV–1, MV, and ME SUPER. It can also be used for manual

The Pentax AF-16 (here mounted on a Pentax ME) pocket-size unit which weighs only 5 ounces including batteries. It can be used in either manual or automatic mode, and features an angle of illumination wide enough to cover the area needed by a 28 mm lens.

operation with these cameras, all other Pentax cameras, and any camera which has a hot-shoe. The AF 200S is another ultra-compact unit, just an inch taller than the AF-16 (this helps you avoid "red eye" in color portraits). The unit is powered by four AA alkaline batteries and you should get about 250 flashes per set of batteries.

When you slide the AF 200S into the MV's hot-shoe, and the exposure-mode dial is on *Auto*, it synchronizes automatically to the proper shutter speed. The X-shaped, flash-ready-indication LED inside the camera's viewfinder becomes operational, and lights when the flash unit is fully charged and ready to fire. Disregard the exposure

LEDs above the *X* because the auto-flash system will provide enough light for the correct exposure. A built-in sensor on the front of the flash adjusts the flash duration automatically. The AF 200S can be synchronized manually with the MV, if the camera's exposure-mode dial is set to *100X*.

The operating procedures, and most of the other characteristics of the AF 200S, are quite similar to those of the AF-16. The AF 200S also features two *f*-stop auto-flash ranges. It has an angle of illumination adequate for 28 mm to 120 mm lenses. There are accessory adapters available for wider-angle and extreme-telephoto lenses.

PENTAX AF–160 ELECTRONIC FLASH

This compact, automatic-thyristor, dedicated, electronic flash unit was added to the Pentax line in the early part of 1980. It is a "dedicated" version of the AF-16. The AF-160 is almost the same size as the AF-16 and weighs only .6 oz. more. The operating ranges of its two automatic settings were increased slightly for maximum depth of field control. It also delivers about 50 more flashes per set of fresh alkaline batteries.

Most important, is the "dedicated" feature of the AF-160. This unit sets the correct synch shutter

speed, and activates the ready-light in the viewfinder, automatically when it is mounted in the hot-shoe of the MV, MV–1, or the ME SUPER. It can be used for standard automatic operation with all other Pentax 35 mm SLR's, and manual operation on these and most other 35 mm SLR's with hot-shoe synchronization.

The AF-16, AF-160, and the AF 200S are quite similar in operation, and have many of the same characteristics. I have prepared a chart to aid you in making your own comparisons.

Front and back views of the Pentax AF 200S flash unit. This is a "dedicated" flash unit which synchronizes automatically with the Pentax MV, MV-1, ME, and ME SUPER cameras.

FEATURES OF ELECTRONIC FLASH UNITS

How does one make a choice from the vast number of portable electronic units that are available today? It would be impossible to cover all models and their features in a book of this size. Instead, here are some basic considerations to help you select the best unit for your particular needs.

There are three size categories and four types of units to choose from. They range from pocket size and medium, hot shoe mount, to large, two-piece, handle-grip units. The four types of operation are manual, automatic, automatic-thyristor, and dedicated.

Guide Numbers

All electronic flash units and flash bulbs have power ratings based on the amount of their light output. These ratings are usually based on use with ASA 25 film, and are known as the unit's Guide Number (GN). (Other methods of designating power output have been used in the past, but the GN has become the standard for comparing the power of portable units today.)

Manual Units

Manual units are the least expensive, but the most inconvenient. Each time you move you have to do calculations and change the f-stop setting of your lens accordingly. The reason for this is that manual units produce the same amount of light each time they are fired. (The same is true of automatic units used in manual mode.) The correct lens-aperture setting is determined by dividing the

PENTAX ELECTRONIC FLASH SPECIFICATIONS

Unit	Size in mm W H D	Weight in oz.	Auto Mode Distance (in feet)	Guide No. (100 ASA)	Batteries Required	Recycle Time *	Flashes per Set	DED. **
AF-16	65 × 78 × 41	3.5	1.5-12 3.3-18	48	2 AA	6 sec.	150	No
AF-160	66 × 81 × 41	5.1	1.6-13 3.3-19.7	48	2 AA	8 sec.	200	Yes
AF-200S	67 × 105 × 60	10	2-11 4.5-23	66	4 AA	6 sec.	250	Yes

*With fresh batteries. Approximate.   **Dedicated operation.

This is the Pentax AF-160 electronic flash unit. It is essentially a "dedicated" version of the earlier AF-16, meaning it synchronizes automatically with certain Pentax camera models, and activates the flash-ready indicator in their viewfinders when recharged.

distance between the flash unit and subject into the GN of the unit. (If the GN is 40 the flash unit is 10 ft. away, set the f-stop to f/4; at five feet the f-stop would be f/8, etc.) To help speed up the selection process many units now have a chart or dial showing the correct f-stops for various ASA film speeds and distances.

Automatic Units

Automatic units cost more, but are well worth the price because they are easy to operate and produce consistent results. They have an electronic sensor that measures the amount of light reflected from the subject instantaneously. They turn the flash off automatically when the sensor registers enough light for correct exposure. This eliminates the need to measure distances and change the f-stop each time you move in relation to the subject. You simply set the f-stop for the ASA of the film you are using, and the flash unit does the rest (as long as you stay within the unit's power range). With different automatic units there is a difference in the number of f-stop settings that can be used, varying from one to five f-stops.

Automatic Thyristor Units

In addition to the convenience of automatic operation, automatic-thyristor units are equipped with special thyristor circuitry which increases the number of flashes you get from a set of batteries, and helps shorten recycling time. Where a conventional automatic unit discharges the extra, unused power generated by the capacitor, thyristor circuitry saves that power. Since less power is needed to generate the next charge, your batteries last longer and recycling takes less time.

Dedicated Units

The most recent advance in electronic flash equipment is the "dedicated" type of automatic-thyristor units. These are designed to be used with a specific automatic 35 mm SLR camera, one that has hot-shoe synchronization and the proper internal electronics. When you mount a fully-charged, "dedicated" unit in the camera's hot-shoe, it activates the flash-ready indicator in the viewfinder. Some units are programmed to set the lens aperture as well.

When the flash-ready indicator in the viewfinder shows that the unit if fully charged, you shoot. Most "dedicated" units have manual operation capability too. They can be used in the manual mode with the specific brand of camera they were designed for, and with other brands of 35 mm SLR's which have hot-shoe synch.

In the summer of 1980 Pentax introduced two new dedicated electronic flash units, as well as the LX camera. These flashes are the AF-280T (shown below), and the AF-400T (shown at left mounted on the LX camera). For further information on these units see Chapter 4.

Convenience Features

A handy feature offered on some units is the sufficient-light indicator, also called a correct-exposure test. This is a device that allows you to fire the flash unit *without exposing the film,* and be sure there is enough light for proper exposure in the automatic mode. You press the open-flash button to trigger the flash, and if the sensor reads enough light for the proper exposure a small diode lights up signaling correct exposure. This is particularly helpful in bounce-flash situations, and when using the auto mode near the maximum operating range of the unit.

Some units also have a tilting light head for bounce flash and many a complete system of accessories, such as filters, longer cords, and remote sensors.

Power Sources

Alkaline Batteries: These are the best choice when you use your flash unit very infrequently, just a few times a year. They usually will provide a minimum of about 100 flashes per set, more when used in an automatic-thyristor unit fairly close to the subject.

Nickel Cadmium Batteries: Although they are higher in initial cost (and some battery packs require a separate battery charger), Nickel Cadmium Batteries (Ni-Cads) can be recharged almost indefinitely. They will pay for themselves many times over if used frequently. Ni-Cads must be kept charged on a regular basis (about once a month) even if they haven't been used. However, recharging times have become very short; one model Ni-Cad battery pack stores enough power for 50 flashes with just a 15 minute charge. This is an exception, but most units need only a few hours recharging time. You will need more than one battery pack (depending on the amount of shooting you plan to do), when you don't have a battery charger with you, or are away from a source of power. One solution is to get a unit that will also accept alkaline batteries and/or can be used with AC current.

High-Voltage Battery Packs: This is a power source for situations that require really fast recycling times, perhaps as short as one half to two seconds, and a great number of flashes. A high-voltage battery pack will provide up to 1,000 flashes in manual mode, and several times that in automatic mode. These over-the-shoulder battery packs are much heavier and more expensive than other power sources, but they are necessary when you need that kind of performance.

AC Power Converter: Barring blackouts, or forgetting to pay the electric bill, your power supply is unlimited with an AC power converter. The only restriction is the length of the extension cord from the wall socket to your electronic flash.

Accessories

Certain electronic flash units have a full system of accessories. Examine each item on the basis of how well it will serve the needs of your kind of photography.

Flash Brackets

If you plan on using a larger-than-pocket-sized flash unit with your camera, a flash bracket is a must. The larger and heavier units can damage your camera's pentaprism housing underneath its hot shoe. Do yourself a favor, and only use the hot shoe mount for the smaller sized units.

Capturing spontaneous moments like this is easy when you have an automatic flash unit like the Pentax AF-16 attached to your camera.

The photograph on the left was taken with the flash mounted on the camera. This method often produces an almost one-dimensional photograph with harsh shadows. The other choice in this situation was to take the shot without the flash and rely on the available light coming from the room's lighting fixtures (right). Since the meter called for an exposure at 1/15 sec. I hoped there wouldn't be too much movement.

Removable Sensors

Most of the pocket-sized electronic flash units have a built-in sensor, but some of the medium-sized or larger automatic units have a removeable sensor. These permit you to use the flash away from the camera. Usually you attach the removable sensor to the camera's hot shoe, and connect it to the flash unit with a sensor cord. The sensor will then measure the flash's power output from the camera position.

Variable-Angle Lenses and Diffusers

The reflectors and lenses used on many electronic flash units are designed to distribute their light over the angle of view covered by a normal 50 mm lens. Variable-angle lenses or diffusers are available to spread or narrow the beam of light, and thus allow the use of wider- or longer-focal length lenses. This lowers the GN when wide-angle coverage is needed, but increases it when the beam is narrowed. Test yourself to see the difference in light output.

SELECTING A FLASH UNIT

The best time to decide which electronic flash unit will fulfill your needs isn't during a fast trip to your local camera store. If you do so, you will probably regret it later because there are many factors to be taken into consideration. Most camera-store salespersons are too busy to devote the time it would require to match your needs against the tremendous number of units being manufactured today.

Since the ultimate responsibility is yours, and it is you who will be using the unit, it would be wise to make a check list to help you compare features. Here is a basic example to help you get started on your own chart:

SPECIFICATION AND FEATURES GUIDE

	Unit 1.	Unit 2.	Unit 3.		Unit 1.	Unit 2.	Unit 3.
ASA 25 Guide Number				Flashes per set of Alkaline Batteries			
Recycling Time				Flashes per set of Ni-Cad Batteries			
Size & Weight				High-Voltage Pack			
Automatic Operation				AC Operation			
Automatic Thyristor				Open-Flash Control			
Multiple *f*-stop Control				Correct-Exposure Test			
Power Supply				Removable Sensor			
Alkaline Batteries				Bounce-Flash Capability			
Ni-Cad Batteries				Guarantee			
Ni-Cad Recharger Time							

USING YOUR ELECTRONIC FLASH

First study the instruction book thoroughly. Keep it handy after you have familiarized yourself with the unit's operation. Although most units operate easily, unless you use them often some of the details become hazy. Carefully install the batteries in the proper position, or follow the instructions for AC use. Attach the PC cord, or mount the unit in the camera's hot shoe, and you are ready to shoot flash pictures. Automatic operation has been covered earlier in this chapter (in the section on the Pentax AF-16 Automatic Electronic Flash).

Manual Operation

The procedure used to determine exposure for manual electronic flash units is the same for automatic or auto-thyristor units when used in manual mode. As stated earlier, flash units and flash bulbs have a GN power rating based on light output. This varies with the speed of the film being used. Most flash units have either a chart or dial with the GNs for various film speeds and distances, to indicate the proper *f*-stop to use.

The basic method used to figure the *f*-stop is to divide the GN of the unit or flash bulb by the

flash-to-subject distance. A GN is just that, a guide. It is based on the light output you can expect in an average-size room with a white ceiling and light-colored walls of average reflectance. Make your own GN tests, and use the results to adjust the aperture or film-speed setting of your unit for the surroundings. When shooting out-

Wide-angle and telephoto adapters for the Pentax AF 200S flash unit.

doors, at night, or in a large room or auditorium where reflectance is at a minimum, open the aperture a full *f*-stop more. In small, all-white, rooms with high reflectance, stop down one full stop.

Camera-Mounted Flash

When a flash unit is mounted on the camera's hot shoe, it provides a far-from-desirable flat-light effect, with dark, harsh shadows. With color film, it also often results in "red eye", that red dot in your subject's eye. To improve flash pictures get an extender accessory with a swivel head which permits raising the unit higher above the hot shoe. This will also allow you to shoot bounce-flash pictures, if your unit doesn't have this capability. If you can, keep your subjects away from light-colored walls, or near a very dark wall, as this will help reduce shadow problems.

Off-Camera Flash

An even better solution to camera-mounted-flash problems is the use of a quick-release flash bracket. The quick-release bracket enables you to remove the flash unit and raise it as high as you wish to get better modeling and a more natural lighting, when there is time.

Bounce Flash

When you want a softer, more pleasing light, try bouncing the flash by pointing your unit towards a reflective surface, such as a ceiling or a wall. You will need a flash unit with a swivel head, or an accessory extender that has an adjustable, ball-socket head.

How do you measure the exposure for this type of lighting? An automatic flash unit with a correct-exposure-test feature will do it for you automatically, but with manual flashes you must do some calculations. Measure the distance from the flash unit to the reflecting surface, then add the distance from that point to the subject, and divide the total into the GN to get the *f*-stop at which to set your lens. With the flash unit angled at 45 degrees the light hitting the ceiling would reflect

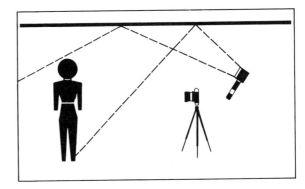

Bounce flash is a technique used to soften or diffuse the harsh light of an electronic flash. It involves bouncing the light from the flash off a ceiling or light-colored wall, rather than aiming the unit directly at the subject.

back onto the subject at a 45-degree angle, forming an inverted V. As a result, in an average room you should open up two stops from the direct-flash-exposure setting. Avoid using bounced light off of colored walls when shooting color film, unless you are experimenting and want the hues reflected on your subject.

Fill-Flash

Outdoor shooting in bright sunlight presents a high-contrast problem because bright highlights and dark shadows are beyond the latitudes of normally-exposed film. This is particularly true of back-lighted subjects, when you want both the background and foreground in visual balance.

Fill-flash is a technique of illuminating (filling) shadow areas with flash. Your shutter speed must be set at either 1/60 or 1/100 sec. for proper synchronization with your electronic flash. This depends on which Pentax you are using (see the earlier flash-synchronization chart). Since an average exposure in bright sunlight with ASA 25 film calls for an aperture of about *f*/16 at 1/60 sec. it is advisable to use slower films (or neutral-density filters) with fill-flash.

First take an available-light exposure reading at the proper shutter speed for flash synch. This will determine your *f*-stop. Divide this *f*-stop into the GN of your flash unit and this will be the distance the flash unit must be from your subject to give an equal balance with the available light. For

Moving lights form interesting patterns and can be used in many ways. A good, steady tripod is a must, since you will need several seconds of exposure in order to get a continuous pattern of lights. This photograph was taken on Panatomic-X film (ASA 32) with an eight-second exposure at f/16.

instance, if the f-stop is f/16 and your GN is 60, the flash unit placed four feet away will equal the sunlight, thus eliminating the shadows completely, and the modeling as well. Since the purpose of using fill-flash is to lighten the shadows, not to remove them, try moving your flash unit back to six, eight, or ten feet. Do some tests to decide which balance you prefer. Most of the time I find that a one-stop difference between the highlights and shadows gives a pleasing balance.

You can also use a clean white handkerchief over the flash head to cut the amount of light delivered, instead of changing the distance. If you do this with an automatic unit, make sure that the handkerchief is securely fastened, and isn't covering the sensor.

Creative Flash Control

In certain circumstances you can make a single flash unit do the work of a studio full of lights by using the open-flash technique. With a little planning, this technique will provide a variety of effects. The prime prerequisites are subjects with little movement, and settings where the existing-light level is low, and where you can use a tripod. One of the basic uses of open flash is to add light to dark areas during a time exposure for the existing light in the scene. The flash unit does not have to be attached to the camera with this technique. You set the camera on "B", open the shutter, fire the flash, and close the shutter after the time exposure has been made. Bounce light can also be effective with this technique.

There are some interesting variations of the open-flash technique that you can try. "Painting with light" is one. It is a way to light huge, dark areas with just one unit. It takes some planning to figure the f-stop you need, so that you can fire the flashes from about the same distance during the time exposure and give the subject enough light where you want it. Care must be taken not to point the flash towards the camera, or it will cause flare spots. If you must fire the light while you are inside the picture area, avoid standing between the camera and the area to be lighted, or you will be silhouetted in the picture. You will need either a long cable release to open and close the shutter each time you flash the scene, or someone to do this for you. The self-timer can be used in smaller areas only, unless you are a track star.

The technique for producing multiple exposures on the same film frame has been described previously. An interesting variation of this is the combination of blurred action with a frozen image or images. Running, jumping, and dancing are some subjects that lend themselves to this technique. To achieve this effect you will need photoflood lights, a dark background, and your electronic flash unit. Light the overall area directly in front of the background with the photo floods. You will want an exposure of about two or three seconds. Be careful to keep the lights from shining directly on the background, or the blurred action will appear washed out.

Divide the *f*-stop needed for the flood-lighted part of the picture into your flash unit's GN to get the distance at which the flash must be fired to freeze action. The best results occur when the flash is fired at a point of key action, with as little light reaching the background as possible. With the floodlights turned on, have your subject start the motion and open the shutter. At the peak action point fire the flash. Close the shutter when the action is completed.

SAFETY PRECAUTIONS

There are some precautions that should be kept in mind when using an electronic flash unit.

1. Asahi recommends turning the power switch *off* when there are long intervals between exposures to save battery power.

2. Although an infrequent occurrence, batteries can leak and cause serious damage. Remove them from the unit when you won't be using it for long periods of time.

3. *Fresh batteries work best.* I keep extra sets in my refrigerator (not the freezer section), along with my color film. Allow at least an hour for them to reach room temperature.

4. Winter can be hazardous to successful picture-taking, since batteries are very sensitive to cold. They do not perform well at freezing temperatures. One solution to this problem is to keep your camera and flash under your jacket or coat, where your body heat will keep them warm. However, be sure to check for moisture condensation on the camera lens when you take it out. Have some lens cleaning tissue handy to wipe the lens clean when necessary.

5. Keep an extra set of batteries with you whenever shooting with flash, and replace the ones in the unit when their recycling time slows.

ALTERNATIVES TO FLASH PHOTOGRAPHY

Though this chapter deals with flash photography, natural-light effects are very appealing and retain the authenticity of the scene. Therefore I am including a brief rundown on getting the most out of today's films.

Boosting Film Speed

High speed films provide the means for photographing a wide range of subject matter in low-light situations, without resorting to artificial light. With special processing both black-and-white and color films can be used at ASA speeds higher than the manufacturer's normal ratings. However, there is some loss in quality with "push" processing and Kodak technical representatives do not recommend boosting film speed more than one stop with color, or two stops with Tri-X black-and-white film. Such processing produces an ASA rating of 800 with Ektachrome 400 color film, a speed undreamed of just a few years ago.

Kodak Color Processing Labs offer a one-stop push service for Ektachrome films at an additional charge. In emergency situations, when there is no other alternative, you can rate the film as much as two or three stops faster than the normal rating, but you will have it processed by a custom photo lab which offers this service.

However, the more the film is pushed, the greater the loss in quality. The size of the grain and the amount of contrast increase, while the resolu-

These photographs were taken with available light. The Tri-X film (ASA 400) was pushed one and a half stops to ASA 1000. There was some loss of quality, but it is not very noticeable.

tion and shadow detail decrease. This is true of both black-and-white and color film. In addition, with color there can be an overall color shift.

Another Professional Lab Service

Many of the custom photo labs have another useful service, the "clip" test. This is particularly useful when you don't have time to bracket exposures, if the whole roll is of one subject, or when the setting and the lighting are similar. The custom lab will cut either the first or last two film frames from your roll and process them carefully to find out how to process the rest of the roll.

INDEX